STRANGE
and
OBSCURE STORIES
of
Washington, DC

STRANGE
and
OBSCURE STORIES
of
Washington, DC

LITTLE-KNOWN TALES ABOUT OUR NATION'S CAPITAL

TIM ROWLAND

Skyhorse Publishing

Skyhorse Publishing books may be purchased in bulk at special discounts for sales promotion, corporate gifts, fund-raising, or educational purposes. Special editions can also be created to specifications. For details, contact the Special Sales Department, Skyhorse Publishing, 307 West 36th Street, 11th Floor, New York, NY 10018 or info@skyhorsepublishing.com.

Skyhorse® and Skyhorse Publishing® are registered trademarks of Skyhorse Publishing, Inc.®, a Delaware corporation.

Visit our website at www.skyhorsepublishing.com.

10 9 8 7 6 5 4 3 2 1

Library of Congress Cataloging-in-Publication Data is available on file.

Cover design by Rain Saukas
Cover images: iStock

Print ISBN: 978-1-5107-2277-4
Ebook ISBN: 978-1-5107-2279-8

Printed in the United States of America

Table of Contents

Preface   vii

CHAPTER 1
Our Founding Speculators Nearly Ruin
Washington's Dream   1

CHAPTER 2
A Storm Saved Washington When Our
Leaders Couldn't   23

CHAPTER 3
Presidential Ambition Ends in Catastrophe   39

CHAPTER 4
Washington Wrestles with Slavery   63

CHAPTER 5
The Best Little Business in Washington   83

CHAPTER 6
Treasury Girls—The Original Rosie Riveters   99

CHAPTER 7

The Most Corrupt Man in a City Full
of Corruption   117

CHAPTER 8

The First Woman in Congress   143

CHAPTER 9

The Tree at National Cathedral Has a Thorny Past   165

Preface

This collection of historical essays is above all meant to be entertaining. If it is also enlightening, well, that cannot be helped.

It is not meant to mirror more traditional, intimidating histories, in all their heavily parsed, foot-noted glory, although the stories presented herein are accurate within what a jury might call a reasonable amount of doubt.

Nor, however, is it meant as snippets of empty-calorie trivia that are so familiar as social media grist. It is hoped that these histories will land somewhere in the middle, engaging the reader with lively but meaningful looks into our past. It is further hoped that readers will be inspired to go on and read more-scholarly works, and in these pages by way of attribution are embedded a number of hints for further reading.

The inspiration for the *Strange and Obscure* series comes from an attempt to win over those who believe history is dull. Certainly, more than a few college students have signed up for a history course that sounds promising, only to be buried alive by an avalanche of dates and troop movements and arcane policy discussions. Of course, these dates and policies are important and provide the backbone of historical knowledge.

But to the more casual student, they can be off-putting and can muffle some of the more human drama that, while perhaps not earth moving, is what makes our history so rich—and entertaining.

The *Strange and Obscure* stories that follow are sometimes obscure in their own right, but just as often they appear as part of a larger, more familiar event. For example, we know about the Burning of Washington in the War of 1812, but maybe not that President James Madison and his inept army were so unpopular that particular night, that if the British hadn't run them out of town, the residents of Washington themselves might have done it for them.

Also, an attempt has been made to place these stories in context with other related events playing out throughout the nation and the world at large at the same time. The tragedy of the USS *Princeton*, to pick one, can only make sense against the backdrop of foreign relations with Britain and Mexico.

The research for these essays is gleaned from published sources, books and historical blogs (many Washington institutions such as the Smithsonian and WETA have fascinating blog sites) as well as collections from the National Archives and period newspapers that are accessible as never before through the miracle of digitalization, including the Library of Congress's *Chronicling America* website.

For a researcher, these sites are almost embarrassingly easy to access, and readers, if they so choose, can do a simple keyword search and scan the letters of George Washington as he becomes ever more irritated with the development of the Federal City, or read the thoughts of Robert Morris as the once-great financier waxed despondent in a Philadelphia debtors' prison.

Since the majority of these stories are from the nineteenth century, a word should be said about nineteenth-century journalism which, counterintuitively perhaps, is not always the best place to go in search of the truth. Papers would typically print rumors as they arrived in the newsroom, more or less correcting them in time as the story evolved. So while the gist of the story would generally be correct, the details cannot always be looked upon as solid evidence. It is, at any rate, what people were being told at the time and what they believed, which in some cases would have been just as meaningful as the actual facts on the ground.

Finally, the primary challenge in any collection of offbeat stories in any city is narrowing down the field of candidates. Washington in particular, home of Congress, has enough weird stuff going on to fill a number of volumes. The stories chosen for this book were picked as offshoots of major historical events that formed a rough time line from the city's planning stages in the late 1700s through the early part of the twentieth century. There might also be a faint bias here to have chosen as to the relevancy, or similarity, of modern affairs. Anyone who reads this, it is hoped, will no longer harbor any doubt about the saw that history repeats itself.

CHAPTER 1

Our Founding Speculators Nearly Ruin Washington's Dream

When glancing at a satellite shot of our nation's capital, the eye comes to rest somewhat naturally on a couple of points of land at the confluence of the Anacostia River and George Washington's beloved Potomac. To the left is Hains Point, an artificial finger of land created from late-nineteenth-century dredging operations and named after the Army engineer Peter Conover Hains, who helped lay the groundwork for the Panama Canal, and also, perhaps more impressively, was the one who finally figured out how to get Washington to stop smelling like a heap of rotting fish.

To the right of Hains Point is a second protuberance commonly known as Buzzard Point. Responsibility for the unfortunate sobriquet falls to Augustine Herman, a Bohemian explorer who prowled the mid-Atlantic coastline in the seventeenth century. If the hulking birds were still around in George Washington's time he did not take it as any sign of bad luck, for on the blunt point of land he envisioned a mighty fortress and bustling commercial waterfront that would amount to a military and economic foundation for a glorious city that would be the envy of the world. It was a grand and plausible plan, but a century later, Buzzard Point was little more than a collection of shacks on spongy ground occupied by poor farmers. Even today, as parks and development have flourished around it, Buzzard Point has remained a somewhat dismal industrial afterthought—to be revived, it's hoped, by a new stadium for the DC United soccer team.

Washington dared to dream big, so it is not a criticism to note that not all his ideas panned out. His idea for a canal extending from the tidewater to the Western territories was too grand in the short run and too tame in the long. He could hardly have seen coming the railroads that put the C&O Canal out of business, so the worst that can be said of the Founder is that he was acting on incomplete information. But there is evidence that Washington's vision for a Federal City that was also a major port and center of commerce was done in not so much by poor planning, but by a handful of men who saw the capital not as a statement of national glory, but as an avenue for personal riches.

In the late 1700s, Washington wasn't the only one with grand designs for Buzzard Point. Lurking in the weeds was a handsome high roller by the name of James Greenleaf. As soon as land in the Federal City (the early name for Washington) was announced for sale, he stepped up and bought the entire locale, which locals took to calling Greenleaf Point, supplanting, temporarily at least, the turkey buzzards that had supplied inspiration for Herman. The blond, hard-partying Greenleaf had a winning disposition, a solid pedigree, an eye for a deal, and, at least at first, credibility. The Greenleaf family (French Huguenots who translated their name to English from the French name Feuillevert) of Massachusetts played an integral role in the American Revolution; James's father announced American independence in 1776 from the balcony of the iconic Old State House in Boston. Among the crowd listening attentively was eight-year-old John Quincy Adams.

Where other members of his family gravitated toward government or more predictable and conservative pursuits, James Greenleaf set his batlike radar on accumulating a vast fortune, which on paper he did. At one point, he owned nearly half of the newly formed Federal City, buying up in excess of eight thousand lots that he hoped to, and sometimes did, flip for three or four times what he paid. He was a great financier or a great bluffer, one of the two, claiming ties to European investors with seemingly limitless capital and an itch for exposure to the American real estate market. Along with his Washington lots, he and his partners also invested in massive tracts of land sight unseen on the American frontier, which at that time fell largely along the eastern foothills of the great Appalachian Mountain chain. Some believe him to have been a classic swindler, and maybe he was, but just as often as he swindled, his syndicate was the swindlee, falling for the sales pitches of frontier hucksters peddling endless stretches of desolate wilderness.

Love him or hate him—and both his contemporaries and historians were and are torn—Greanleaf represented a swath of

American life that is with us to this day. Two centuries before Donald Trump, and *The Wolf of Wall Street*, James Greenleaf made the mold. In this he was not alone, of course. Many of the Founders who are quite properly idolized today had the Rights of Man at the top of their to-do list, just after the chore of amassing enormous personal wealth. Many of these men bet and failed with equal splendor. Robert Morris, Greenleaf's most famous partner, is known for his role as one of the premier financiers of the American Revolution. But other than that, Morris was up to his elbows in most any enterprise imaginable, including the slave trade. (In one of those delicious ironies of colonial America, Morris the government agent agitated for taxation of the slave trade; Morris the private individual dodged Pennsylvania slave tariffs by docking his slave ship in Delaware.)

These early land speculators maintained fascinating relationships with each other, often building alliances with those whom they were simultaneously stabbing in the back. In the end, it all came crashing down, leaving the speculators either humbled, ruined, dead, or all three. And they almost took the Federal City down with them—although in this, they had considerable help from the political sector.

Today, we rightly view the creation of Washington, DC, as a success story; but in 1800, it wouldn't have seemed that way at all. The first inhabitant of the executive mansion, John Adams, dropped his satchels in horror when he got a glimpse of the locale he was supposed to call home. It was half-finished, reeking of wet horsehair plaster and plopped in the middle of a shantytown of construction workers, Adams wondered how he was going to break the news to Abigail, who was used to the finer things in life. "Not a single thing about Washington exuded the atmosphere of a city," wrote Andrea Wulf in the book *Founding Gardeners*. "Quails perched in the bushes, bullfrogs serenaded lonely riders . . . Pennsylvania Avenue was hidden by a thorny veil of briars and described by one contemporary as impenetrable."

It was a mess that, in hindsight, was totally predictable—because the city was the product of one of those political compromises that manages to incorporate the very worst aspects of all sides—and opened the door for speculators who did not have the city's best interests at heart. To anyone familiar with today's political stalemates, the petty, pigheaded, and unproductive arguments that flared over the city's foundation would have been instantly recognizable. And this scrap involved some of our most cherished national heroes, so for those who despair at current political conditions, at least it can be said that we come by it honestly.

The Federalists, including Washington and Alexander Hamilton, wanted a capital city of power and swagger. This horrified Republicans like James Madison and Thomas Jefferson who thought that our capital should be tucked away in some backwater in order to downplay the importance of government. Jefferson sketched out his idea for a federal city, a humble grid that was only slightly more complex than a game of tic-tac-toe. So while the Federalists wanted New York City, the Virginians had something in mind that would have been more along the lines of *Mayberry R.F.D.*

Then there was the whole North versus South conflict, whereby Southerners absolutely refused to consider a capital located in any of the burgeoning Northeastern cities. Hamilton was already scheming to centralize the nation's money, and building a federal treasury in his New York stomping grounds would have been just a little too convenient. But, lacking any meaningful population or industry at the time, putting a capital in the South struck Northerners as about as sensible as building a livery on the moon. In the end, a 1790 compromise allowed Hamilton to consolidate the states' Revolutionary War debts under a federal umbrella, while, in a nod to Jefferson, the capital was established below the Mason-Dixon Line on the Potomac River, somewhere between Georgetown and Williamsport, Maryland. The exact location would be President Washington's call.

The upshot was predictable. By announcing that it would build a city from scratch, the government effectively put out a clarion call for anyone who happened to be interested in participating in get-rich-quick schemes, the sketchier the better. Some stretch of godforsaken wasteland was, in theory at least, about to get incredibly valuable, and men began buying up land up and down the Potomac and then lobbying Washington to pick their newly acquired ground for the capital city.

Meanwhile, the ripples that fanned out from the Jefferson-Hamilton compromise (said to have occurred over an impromptu dinner between the two, at which the chief facilitator was a sizable cask of wine) were beginning to fray old alliances and shatter those that had never been too strong to begin with. Democrats today claim Jefferson as one of their own, while Republicans claim Lincoln; but only the devil and Broadway claim Hamilton. Even back then he was a convenient target. Jefferson came to believe he had been hoodwinked by his hated rival—which he probably was. Jefferson's victory, the location of a city, was largely cosmetic, while Hamilton institutionalized central finance, the bane of small-government advocates to this day.

History has treated Washington far more kindly, excusing the same centrist outlook for which Hamilton has been tarred and feathered. For all his father-of-the-country laurels, George Washington at root was a man not of government, but of agriculture and commerce. His heart, mind, and home—and wallet—were on the Potomac.

Washington saw the new capital's site as an opportunity for both great public and private works. He would have been disappointed to learn that his namesake city would become known as a hotbed of lawyers and lobbyists and not as a serious, major port such as Baltimore, New York, or New Orleans. But at the time, it seemed that politics was playing into the president's hands. Congress's Residence Act of 1790 allowed Washington to choose the specific site from this general region, and to carve out up to one hundred square miles for the city. Washington aggressively took every inch: this brand-new city would be the size of all of occupied London, and bigger that all the great northeastern American cities combined—with only a handful of lawmakers, saloon keepers, and moo-cows to fill it. The Capitol and executive mansion were sited a mile apart, which, considering the remote locale, was a bit like building a house in which the bathroom was a block away from the kitchen. For decades, Washington was less of a cohesive city that a patchwork of loosely confederated neighborhoods. (Contrary to popular lore, Washington was not built on a swamp, although developers—who would have stared blankly at the modern ideas of storm water management and sediment control—conspired to turn it into one.)

As part of the Residence Act, a three-man commission was to oversee the development of the city, a job made more difficult by the federal government's lack of taxing power. To get around this, the commissioners cooked up what sounded like a plausible plan: The land for the city would be subdivided into thousands of building lots, and the proceeds from the sale of these lots would pay for the government buildings, infrastructure, public fountains, and ornamentation that would make up the backbone of the District. The one thing they neglected to work out was where the thousands of people to buy the lots were supposed to come from—even New York City at that point in time had scarcely more than thirty-three thousand residents, and it, at least, was a viable port. Nevertheless, in 1791, to much anticipation and fanfare, the commission put a large swath of lots to auction—and had all of thirty-one takers. At an average price of $265 (about $6,600 today), the resulting revenue was obviously a few columns shy of a shining city on a hill.

No one was quite sure what to do. Without residents and without revenues, there could be no Federal City, so pressure mounted on the commission to find someone to take these parcels off their hands.

Speculators, and James Greenleaf in particular, began to smell the sweet scent of desperation, in which he could buy the lots on the cheap and at such quantity that he would one day be able to flip them at considerable profit after he had cornered the market and driven up demand.

Greenleaf began his play by courting the alpha male of the Residence Act commission, Thomas Johnson, the first governor of Maryland who served a brief stint on the Supreme Court. Greenleaf bragged about his connections to Dutch financiers and on the side helped Johnson invest in some Western Maryland properties, with the idea of buttering up the notoriously persnickety pol. He scarcely had to bother; with few other takers in evidence, the commission was eager, perhaps too eager to do a deal. Those who didn't know Greenleaf were thrilled with his interest in the Federal City, and his ostensible connections to virtually unlimited capital. Those who did know Greenleaf sat back and waited for the other boot to drop.

The speculator did indeed have a connection to Dutch financiers. The first popular anecdote about Greenleaf concerned his 1788 marriage to a Dutch woman with a never-ending name: The Baronesse Antonia Cornelia Elbertine Scholten van Aschat et Oud-Haarlem. Greanleaf, on a business trip to sell American financial instruments to the Dutch, spotted her virtually the second he stepped off the ship in Amsterdam, and it should surprise no one that she also happened to, by pure luck, be the product of an eminent family of Dutch bankers. The marriage was Greenleaf's first order of business during a four-year stint in the Netherlands selling American bonds and bank stock. His business transactions were extremely productive, but his marriage less so. Greenleaf's story, according to his biographer, Allen C. Clark, was that the couple experienced love at first sight, leading to a lustful tryst without any of the traditional courtship, candy, flowers and such. This version of the facts would imply that Greenleaf was later blindsided by the happy coincidence that, aside from being the light of his life, she also happened to have some serious ties to the Dutch financial world.

Anyway, wouldn't you know that after his banking contacts had been established, Greenfield realized that Baroness Antonia Cornelia Elbertine etc. was not his soul mate after all, and he booked passage home to make use of his new cash accounts and prospective lines of credit. It was on a trip home to America, however, that he received word that the baroness was pregnant; putting his own feelings second, he raced back to Amsterdam to be at her side. On his arrival, he learned that no child was in the offing—he was told that his wife had miscarried, but a servant let it slip that the whole story was a hoax cooked up by the lonely wife in order to lure her husband back home. This discovery was followed by tearful confessions, suicide attempts, separations, and all manner of drama amidst the tulips, culminating with Greenleaf's return to the states. Back home, and suitably soured on the whole idea of matrimony, he took up residence in Rhode Island—at that time something of a Reno, Nevada, of the East—long enough to obtain a quickie divorce.

This unpleasantness behind him, or so he thought, Greenleaf was in the Federal City in September 1793 to watch George Washington and his fellow masons lay the cornerstone of the US Capitol. With both Residence Act commissioner Thomas Johnson and a supposed million dollars of Old World cash in his pocket, Greenfield was ready to deal. Though the commission had set a prospective price per lot of between $250 and $300, Greenleaf's willingness to buy in bulk allowed him to insist in the bargain-basement price of $66 each for three thousand parcels—even so, time would show that Greenleaf was overpaying. And it still didn't solve the problem of identifying thousands of potential home and shop owners who would be willing to buy into what was essentially an urban experiment on the banks of a deserted river plain. There would be a handful of bureaucrats, laborers, and government support-service workers fluttering about the capital, but at that time they hardly would fill a city of one hundred square miles.

This was not Greenleaf's concern, since his customers were not going to be the clerks and coal jockeys who would populate the town, but Dutch investors looking to make a buck. He bought another three thousand lots at eighty dollars each, and even with his added commitment to build a handful of brick houses each year and a promise to loan the commissioners enough cash each month to keep their public-improvement plans somewhat alive, a few interested parties began to smell a rat.

George Washington was initially pleased with the deal—Greenleaf had gotten a bargain, the president wrote to his secretary Tobias Lear in 1793, but given the trouble the commissioners had experienced in interesting anyone else, the deal was needed to "give facility to the operations" of the nascent city.

But within two years Washington had become disillusioned, bordering on bitter. Somehow, Greenleaf had been able to scrounge up some Englishmen who were interested in participating in the experiment, and also willing to pay the full retail price for the lots, not to the Residence commission, but to Greenleaf. An irritated Washington wrote to Residence Act commissioner Daniel Carroll in 1795:

You will recollect no doubt that I yielded my assent to Mr. Greenleaf's first proposition to purchase a number of lots in the Federal City . . . because at that time seemed to be in a stagnant state, and something was necessary to put the wheels in motion again. To the second Sale which was made to him, my repugnance was greater, in as much as the necessity for making it was not so apparent to my view— and because another thing had become quite evident—Viz: that he was speculating deeply—was aiming to monopolize deeply, and was thereby laying the foundation of immense profit to himself and those with whom he was concerned.

Carroll was a friend, business associate, and fellow Founding Father, but none of that spared him from Washington's barbed pen. Although Greenleaf was able to flip the lots at several times what he paid, the commission could only move them at a deep discount. "Lately a gentleman from England has paid, or is to pay, £50,000 for 500 lots," he wrote. "Will it not be asked why are speculators to pocket so much money? Are not the Commissioners as competent to make bargains?"

But Greenleaf, it turned out, was doing more with the Federal City lots than simply flipping them at a profit. He was using their value, or perceived value, to fund even more complex financial schemes. It is only slight exaggeration to say that the modern-day tranches, credit default swaps, and collateralized debt obligations that led to the global financial meltdown of 2008 were a study in simplicity compared to the tangled bird's nest of complexities that the Founding Speculators employed. They would borrow heavily on lands they owned (on paper at least) to buy more land, mortgage the new land, use the proceeds as a down payment on even more land, lose the original land to foreclosure and touch off a hopelessly snarled court battle among their creditors—only to emerge and circuitously reclaim former property of theirs at auction for pennies on the dollar.

Using this technique, Greenleaf continued to sop up land like a sponge—more than two thousand acres on the Anacostia River at Buzzard Point, three hundred acres in Alexandria and 1,240 lots in the "Town of George." By 1794, the chances that any given structure in the "city" (loosely defined) was owned by Greenleaf were one in three. Meanwhile, he continued to be active in Upstate New York, where land transactions were, if anything, muddier than the ones in the District. Greenleaf's fingerprints even extend to the deadly feud between Aaron Burr and Alexander Hamilton, to wit: Burr had essentially been duped into purchasing 210,000 New York acres that he could not afford, and as was his custom, Greenleaf magically appeared to, for a price, help Burr out of his troubles. Greenleaf couldn't afford the purchase price either, but no matter, he took possession of the deed on credit and immediately mortgaged the land to pay for a cargo of tea. Default was the obvious outcome, and Burr was left holding the bag. The man who had sold the property hired attorney and former Treasury Secretary Hamilton to sue Burr and the relationship between the two spiraled downward from there.

The situation also illustrates why it was, and is, so hard to track Greenleaf's financial dealings with any degree of confidence. Greenleaf's biographer, Allen C. Clark, for all intents and purposes, simply dropped back and punted: "To dissipate disappointment on the outset I confess inability to make a clear and concise exposition of the entanglement of Greenleaf. I believe for an exact exhibition the data does not exist." Of his affairs with his business partners Robert Morris and John Nicholson (a tightly wound analytics guy who had been run out of his former office as Pennsylvania comptroller on suspected financial malfeasance), he concluded "they can be likened unto a fabric so compactly and complexly woven as to be beyond finite skill to separate and sort the threads."

But no matter how tightly these threads might have been woven, at some point it all would start to unravel. The best the partners could hope for was to delay the inevitable; and perhaps before it all went to pot, one of their speculations would hit a home run and pay off the debt that was accumulating to a staggering degree. The key was to stall for time, and they found an original way to do it.

Today, most casual securities traders are familiar with REITs, real estate investment trusts, which are agencies that assemble similar properties into one company and sell shares of the trust in the open market. But the biggest REIT in American history had nothing to do with hotels or assisted-living apartments. It was instead called the North American Land Company, a trust created by Greenleaf, Morris, and Nicholson that held an astonishing six million acres from New York to Georgia.

Morris in particular had never met a square foot of real estate that he didn't like. The financier of the American Revolution firmly believed that he could buy vast tracts for pennies an acre and sell them at a dizzying profit to the waves of incoming Europeans who had never owned real estate and would be rabid for the opportunity. It was a solid idea in theory, and had Morris lived to be two hundred years old, he might have realized his dream. But even for the balance of the nineteenth century there would have been little market for the aptly named pine barrens in Georgia or the mountainous regions of New York that mapmakers at the time were labeling as "Howling Wilderness."

Whether rural land or (potentially) urban land, Morris did not discriminate. And Greenleaf for his part was just as happy to flip lots to his partner as to the Europeans, particularly since the property in Washington was becoming ever more difficult to move. As early as 1795, Federal City investor Thomas Law—an East India Company reformer who was one of the few to rub elbows with Greenleaf and more or less survive financially—sensed disaster. In a letter to Greenleaf he wrote that Morris "appropriates his funds to distant objects and diverts his funds and the labor of the people from works more immediately productive. He borrows at a dreadful interest and sells disadvantageously like a desperate gambler to recover what he has lost—he has I know great resources, but no fortune can support his constant drains." Eventually Law would come to realize that it was Greenleaf himself who was helping to feed Morris's addiction.

Law was correct; mortgages on top of mortgages could only stand for so long, and the syndicate was in desperate need of cash. And if liquidity were the problem, the North American Land Company would be the answer. Greenfield, Morris, and Nicholson swept every toxic holding on their books into the trust and sold shares of this dubious outfit to investors. It was remarkably similar to the way bankers in the financial crisis repackaged subprime loans as high-quality debt, selling it to investors at the same time they were placing side bets that the bogus financial instruments were, in fact, bogus.

The Founding Speculators seem not to have been able to help themselves, so focused were they on the plan to corner the market on American real estate. That the continent was so vast that no monopoly on land was remotely feasible did not cross anyone's mind. They honestly believed they were just one more deal, one more line of credit, one cash infusion way from fantastic wealth that had only been known, ironically enough, to the kings whose grasp they had done so much to escape.

In the end, the Founding Speculators were done in by their own sleight of hand. Due to their real estate shenanigans, a clear land title in America became such a rare commodity that honest investors at home and abroad were too worried about getting burned to take the risk. So too had they learned that much American land was too infertile, too mountainous, or too isolated to be of value. Greenleaf and Co. were saddled with infinite inventory but no buyers, and the speculative American land bubble burst with a sound that was heard across two continents. When the War of the First Coalition broke out in Europe, the last great hope of the trio that everything would work out all right in the end was extinguished. If Greenfield had ever had a blank check from Dutch bankers it was gone now, and among those left holding the bag were those who had had such high hopes for the Federal City.

Historian Bob Arnebeck doubted that war made much difference, although he dryly suggests it's as good an excuse as any: "Perhaps the matter should be left at that because then it could be said that this was the only war in history that retarded the growth of Washington, DC. But since Baltimore and New York were booming because of the war, it's fairer to say only that the war was the first excuse to cover up mismanagement and cupidity on the part of those charged with developing the city."

When the bottom fell out, it was like a game of musical chairs with no seats to be had for anyone. Those who had gambled the most heavily on American lands almost invariably wound up in debtors' prison, including Greenleaf, Morris, and Nicholson. Nicholson—whose most salient advice to Morris as the noose tightened was to drink heavily—died in the Philadelphia jail where they all wound up, compulsively writing letters to the end, to anyone he thought might listen.

The most poignant of all was Morris, who was regarded as one of the greats of American history. Morris escaped debtor prison at first, only through a quirk in the law. Debtors had to be served court papers in person (and couldn't be served at all on Sundays) before they could be imprisoned, so Morris simply sequestered himself in the Philadelphia estate he dryly named "Castle Defiance" and refused to come out. Morris was free, but not really. Twelve million dollars in arrears, he finally surrendered and was thrown into debtors' prison in 1798 where he languished for three years before Congress—shamed by the awkward jailing of a man who had given so much to the cause—passed temporary bankruptcy protections that afforded the patriot his freedom.

"To think," mused historian James J. Reis, "someone who was once the wealthiest man in America, now in his sixties, someone who signed the two most important documents in history, the United States Constitution and the Declaration of Independence, was now off to fend for himself in prison."

For most, debtors' prison was a dismal place, but for Morris, who still had assets at his disposal, it was somewhat better. He was able to furnish his cell in rather grand fashion, and even entertained George Washington one evening for dinner. Still, his frustration was evident in a letter to Nicholson. Signing his name Bob Morris, he grumbled over his inability to control his own fate: "I do not feel much disposed to pass my time in writing or copying letters that end in—nothing. When there is real business, I will endeavor to attend to it." Morris stewed at the Prune Street institution where he was imprisoned for more than three years. Five years later he was dead, the life of a great American ending sadly, with a whimper.

Greenleaf was somewhat luckier, as he always seemed to be. Imprisoned a year prior to Morris, he petitioned for relief under Pennsylvania's insolvency laws, only to have his dubiously earned divorce come back to bite him. Those whom he had filched in the past helpfully pointed out to the court that the divorce decree he had obtained in a Rhode Island courtroom meant that he couldn't possibly be considered a Pennsylvania resident deserving of its legal protections. A small, petty victory, perhaps, but to his creditors, as they swilled their rum at the local publick house, it had to feel good.

Meanwhile, in the Federal City, Greenleaf was acquiring even more enemies, as investors learned that they had been sold a bill of goods. Lots that Greenleaf had mortgaged and later sold (including some to Morris and Nicholson) were repossessed out from under the ostensible owners, who had themselves as often as not used them as collateral for some other harebrained speculation. For all the careful, meticulously orchestrated plans of George Washington and the Residency commissioners, it was as if someone had blown thousands of deeds into the air with an industrial fan, allowing any number of ne'er-do-wells to catch as catch can.

The city's commissioners obviously wanted to repossess and resell the lots, but Arnebeck boils down the considerable problem therein, which was that "consequently a perspective buyer faced a situation in which the commissioners, the trustees of (Philadelphia creditors), Greenleaf, Georgetown creditors of Morris and Nicholson, and the Bank of Columbia, not to mention the sheriff, for various causes of indebtedness on the part of Greenleaf, Morris and Nicholson, might contest and win possession of the lots the commissioners were trying to sell."

In other words, any piece of paper representing itself as a clean title would have spontaneously combusted. Naturally, there's little value to contested deeds, and Arnebeck notes that properties that George Washington had hoped would fetch upwards of $300 in the 1790s were only fetching $47 a half century later.

It was at that time, fifty years after George Washington had held out such high hopes for the city, that it was paid a visit by British author and journalist Charles Dickens, who in his travelogue did not pull any punches:

It is sometimes called the City of Magnificent Distances, but it might with greater propriety be termed the City of Magnificent Intentions; for it is only on taking a bird's-eye view of it from the top of the Capitol that one can at all comprehend the vast designs of its projector, an aspiring Frenchman. Spacious avenues that begin in nothing, and lead nowhere; streets, mile long, that only want houses, roads, and inhabitants; public buildings that need but a public to be complete; and ornaments of great thoroughfares, which only lack great thoroughfares to ornament— are its leading features.

No one would be in Washington if he didn't have to be, Dickens thought. A small handful of magnificent government buildings were juxtaposed against a macabre collection of shanties and waste lots that the Founding Speculators had left in their wake. Looking out of the window of his shabby boarding house, Dickens gazed upon "a long, straggling row of houses, one story high, terminating, nearly opposite, but a little to the left, in a melancholy piece of waste ground with frowzy grass, which looks like a small piece of country that has taken to drinking, and has quite lost itself."

The Founding Speculators, five decades prior, had apathetically threw up a house or business here and there, mainly to keep the commissioners off their backs and convince investors that the city was about to explode in growth, making a fortune for one and all. Greenleaf, for example, began to erect twenty buildings on Greenleaf Point, in a neighborhood inspirationally known as the "Twenty Buildings." But he never finished them, and twenty-five years after construction was initiated, the community was a dismal ruin.

But there are still today a few fragments of Greenleaf's legacy that still survive, including the Duncanson-Cranch House at 468–470 N Street SW and the Thomas Law House, 6th Street, near N street SW. Also surviving is Wheat Row, today 1315, 1317, 1319, and 1321 4th Street SW, the greater miracle perhaps being that the small row of undersized townhouses ever got built in the first place. The design and construction were poor and Greenfield (surprise) refused to pay the builder, James Clark, who partnered with the flamboyant developer and suffered a nervous breakdown for his trouble.

In the end, Greenleaf's salad days in Washington were remarkably brief. By 1797 he was bankrupt, an event he celebrated by taking a wealthy heiress as his bride—a handsome woman named Ann Penn Allen (granddaughter of the founder of Allentown, Pennsylvania) who, along with her looks was smart enough to require the eighteenth-century version of a prenup before giving her hand to Greenleaf. The marriage was by all accounts civil enough, although the two wound up living apart—Greenleaf in Washington where his presence was so often required in court, and Ann in Allentown, which she regarded as less ugly and more civilized than the city of her husband's creation.

Unlike Morris and Nicholson, Greenfield lived a long and relatively comfortable and contented life in his postspeculative years. He did what most failed American entrepreneurs do—he became a consultant, and lived off his speaking fees and his wife's fortune. He enjoyed his gardens, his books, and a few close friends and lived to be seventy-eight, dying in 1843.

His legal legacy lived for some time after that, and as the 1800s came to a close the courts were still trying to untangle his land and financial holdings. His name appeared prominently in thirteen cases that were argued before the Supreme Court and astonishingly enough, Greenleaf at least partially prevailed in all of them. In this way too, he resembled today's financiers, creating chaos yet seldom suffering the indignity of being held accountable. Had he lived in modern times he would have had a movie made about him. A rogue, scoundrel, and swindler? Yes. But, it can be argued that Washington has survived worse.

Chapter 2

A Storm Saved Washington When Our Leaders Couldn't

In 1803, in order to help pay for his war machine, Napoleon Bonaparte sold the Louisiana Territory to the United States. He felt no particular sense of loss; the Emperor assumed he could always conquer it later should he want it back.

But he never had the chance. A decade of warfare found him in the snows of Russia, where five hundred thousand of the six hundred thousand soldiers that he marched with to Moscow didn't return. A coalition of nations defeated him at Leipzig and marched on Paris, where he abdicated in the spring of 1812.

Four thousand miles away, in Washington, DC, it was unlikely that residents, when they eventually received the news, would have seen any potential cause and effect between Napoleon's surrender and their own pursuit of happiness.

Wiser American statesmen, however, might have understood the implications. Britain had been fighting a cataclysmic war on the continent, affording it few resources to allocate to the Americas, where the pesky little brother of a nation remained a burr under the British saddle—and vice versa. The United States had won the Revolution, but to the newly minted Americans it seemed as if Britain hadn't gotten the message.

Britain, for example, continued its practice of impressing sailors on merchant ships for service in the British Navy, even those sailors who considered themselves to be naturalized Americans. The Crown's view was once a Brit, always a Brit, and upwards of ten thousand "American" sailors were captured and forced into duty on His Majesty's warships. The British were also restricting trade and making mischief out West, supporting Native Americans fighting to protect their lands against westward expansion of the frontier. The Indians would have had a right to be suspicious; they'd been treated terribly at the hands of the British in the past, and indeed, the proffered "help" was little more than a strategy to block American expansion into lands on which the British had designs in the Pacific Northwest.

The War of 1812 was puffed up as the "second war of independence" against the British, although it was nothing of the sort. The war was about territory, with Americans pushing both to the west, where it had success, and to the north, where it didn't. Americans were repeatedly repulsed in Quebec and Ontario, and even to this day, Canadians are still pretty chesty about it. (It celebrated the bicentennial anniversary of the War of 1812, which was scarcely noticed in the States, with a three-year commemoration.)

Even the American's successes north of the border would eventually come back to haunt them. On April 27, 1813, an American force landed on the shores of Lake Ontario at the provincial capital York, site of present-day Toronto. In military terms, there was little reason to take the lightly defended town, save for symbolism or the hollow glory that accompanies, say, beating a seven-year-old in a game of chess. Even so, the battle was not without its costs, resulting as it did in the deaths of several American officers including the great explorer of the Rocky Mountains, Zebulon Pike.

Pike and thirty-seven other Americans were killed by flying debris when the British quietly abandoned the fort that was defending the town, and set a fuse leading to the fort's powder magazine. If the Americans felt this was dirty pool, it perhaps contributed to their treatment of the city, where they burned government buildings and engaged in extensive looting, taking, among other things, the ceremonial mace of parliament, which remained in American hands for 121 years until Franklin D. Roosevelt, as a goodwill gesture, finally gave it back.

But when the Napoleonic Wars in Europe ended in April 1814, and the British turned their full attention to America, the rude treatment of York still would have been relatively fresh in their minds, and they would have been keeping an eye out for an opportunity at payback. As the British veterans of the European wars set sail for American shores, a young British soldier and divinity student named George Robert Gleig relished the chance at "chastening an enemy than whom none had ever proved more vindictive or ungenerous."

Gleig was in a brigade of toughened British fighters under Major General Robert Ross who sailed for Bermuda and then to Washington after the cessation of hostilities in Belgium. Ross rendezvoused with Rear Admiral George Cockburn, who had been harassing Chesapeake Bay settlements (bad) and trying to goad slaves into rising up in arms against their masters (worse). Cockburn correctly guessed Washington's vulnerability, but initially the mission seemed less intent on defeating the Americans than it was on giving them a good spanking to make up for the outrages and atrocities perpetuated against Canadians around the Great Lakes. Rather than outright victory, Ross's orders effectively were to make a nuisance of himself and force the Americans to divert men and money away from more critical theaters of the war.

As Ross made his way up the coast, President James Madison and his cabinet kept a sharp on his progress and speculated on his intentions. An attack on the nation's capital was all but ruled out because, frankly, Washington was such a dump at that point in its history that bombing it would be a senseless waste of perfectly good shells. Madison had forgotten, perhaps, that the destruction of the provincial capital of York was a relatively fresh wound that the British felt was still worth avenging. But whatever the thought process, a British attack on the capital in the summer of 1815 was undeniably something for which the American military was completely unprepared. Despite months of advance warning, there were no militia call-ups, no fresh defensive earthworks, and no indication that those officers in charge of defending the capital had done much of anything at all, save for strolling around to get a general lay of the land.

No one was more puzzled than the British themselves, who staged on Tangier Island in the Chesapeake Bay, and—after sailing as far as they could up the Patuxent River—marched unimpeded on Washington from the northeast. In the Revolution, the American's tactics had confounded the orderly British. Rigid lines and strict discipline were virtually useless against American militiamen who hid behind rocks and trees and acted more as freelance sharpshooters then a cohesive fighting force.

So the British assumed their upcoming campaign would be more of the same: The Americans would cut down trees to block their path, dig trenches, destroy bridges and then pick off the Redcoats one by one when they stopped to clear the road. On the morning of August 24, forty-five hundred British regulars were up early, marching tentatively on a horrid road through a thick Maryland wood. It would have been child's play to fell a few trees and slow the column to the point that the Redcoats would have been sitting ducks for sniper fire. But that didn't happen.

Still, it looked as if the heavy, humid August air would do what the Americans didn't. The soldiers had been protected from the sun by a thick tree canopy in the morning, but when they broke out into cleared fields, the heat became oppressive, with temperatures approaching one hundred degrees. More and more soldiers began to fall behind, until the column marching on Washington was reduced by half. The officers were finally forced to stop at a creek, where the soldiers splashed in water as they waited for the stragglers to catch up. As the sweating, red-faced men tried to summon a second wind, they had to be wondering whether, by the time they reached enemy resistance, they would have any energy left for the fight.

Everything was, or should have been, in the American's favor. They outnumbered the British two to one. They were defending their nation's capital, while the enemy was simply there to create a nuisance. But despite the enormous stakes, the Americans, led by a lawyer by trade, Brigadier General William H. Winder demonstrated a stunning lack of urgency. "With the enemy nearing the capital by both land and water, American military intelligence was so inadequate, and staff work so nonexistent, that when a scouting party formed to ascertain the position of the redcoats, Secretary of State James Monroe saddled up and led it," wrote Daniel Walker Howe in *What Hath God Wrought: The Transformation of America, 1815–1848.* Except, having forgotten his spyglass, a key implement of military intelligence in those days, Madison made poor work of it. On the battlefield, the Americans were led by the floridly incompetent Brigadier General William H. Winder, a political appointee whose reputation so preceded himself that many residents of Washington fled before it had even been confirmed that the British were near.

Along with their fear of the enemy, they were also sorely afraid that Cockburn might be successful in his efforts to encourage Maryland slaves to revolt. While they didn't revolt in the strictest sense, several hundred did run away and join the British force, where they acquitted themselves well.

While the Americans did not play to their strengths during the British advance, they did have the time and wherewithal to position themselves well on high ground at the small commercial center of Bladensburg, nine miles from downtown Washington, where they tried to make a stand. Historians differ on the American performance at Bladensburg. Harry

Ammon called it "the greatest disgrace ever dealt to American arms," while in the opinion of J.C.A. Stagg, it was "the most humiliating episode in American history." The truth is probably somewhere in between.

The two armies discovered each other in the way that they commonly did in those days—by the clouds of dust rising skyward behind a ridge line kicked up by thousands of boots and hooves. The British rounded a bend in the road to see the Americans in three lines, two ready to fight, one in reserve. They were properly anchored on the flanks, a tributary of the Potomac on one end, a deep ravine on the other. Even better, in theory, the British had to cross a bridge before engaging in battle, a choke point that should have been easy to defend.

Ross sent a light brigade across the bridge, and the first shot of American artillery, perfectly placed, wiped out an entire company of Redcoats. For Winder's men, it would be the highpoint of the day. For some reason, the American gunners lost the range after their initial volley. The light brigade streamed across the bridge, crouched behind whatever cover the men could find and took aim. James Madison later remarked that he had no idea the difference between militia (armed civilians, basically) and professional soldiers could be so great. The British regulars, calm under fire, sent one volley into the American lines, and that was about all it took. American casualties were amazingly light that day, because most outran the projectiles that were sent in their direction. They tossed away their loaded muskets as they ran. Bewildered British soldiers looked at each other and shrugged.

The American militia might be cut some slack, if only because they had been asked to fight in a way to which they were not accustomed. In the traditional European method of warfare in that day—where two lines of men faced off and fired at each other—accuracy was not essential. If the shot were a little right or a little left, it hardly mattered. What was essential was teamwork, something that was not necessarily a component of American individualism, or among shooters used to deliberately firing from trees or behind rocks. Lining them up shoulder to shoulder to elbow each other as they loaded and shot was well out of their comfort level.

Winder's men quit the field—if not at a full sprint, close to it—and left it in the quite incapable hands of Brigadier General Tobias Stansbury, whom Winder told to hold Baldensburg if he could, destroy the bridge out of town if he couldn't, and don't forget to write. As a military officer, Stansbury might not have known much, but he knew when he'd been abandoned. As historian John R. Elting wrote, "Lacking the least desire to emulate the Spartans at Thermopylae, he roused his groggy command about 3:00 a.m. and headed toward Washington, forgetting to destroy the Bladensburg bridge behind him."

The Scotsman soldier Gleig later wrote, ". . . had they conducted themselves with coolness and resolution it is not conceivable how the battle could have been won. But the fact is that with the exception of a party of sailors from the gunboats under the command of Commodore [Joshua] Barney, no troops could behave worse than they did. The skirmishers were driven in as soon as attacked, the first line gave way without offering the slightest resistance and the left of the main body was broken within half an hour after it was seriously engaged."

This is not to say there were no heroes in the War of 1812 as it is understood in the popular imagery of today. One is

General Andrew "Old Hickory" Jackson, renowned in song for winning the Battle of New Orleans, which was actually fought after the war's conclusion due to slow communications of the day. Another is Francis Scott Key who penned the words that became the National Anthem as the British were repulsed in Baltimore. And a third is Dolley Madison snatching the iconic Lansdowne portrait of George Washington from the clutches of the torch-wielding British.

As is frequently the case with our most treasured national anecdotes, the story of Dolley and George comes with a number of asterisks and caveats. What's now acknowledged is that Dolley didn't save the Lansdowne portrait at all; it was a copy, one of several that Gilbert Stuart made of his original. This is easy to prove, because in the copies (including Dolley's) he painted in minor errors, as on a book in the background with "United 'Sates' of America" printed on the spine. National lore holds that Dolley—with the mansion aflame and the British beating at the door—ordered the painting cut from its frame screwed to the wall. Dissatisfied with the expediency of the project, she herself cut the canvas free and assigned it to a pair of close family friends for safeguarding.

In truth, the British were at that point only rumored to be on their way, and the petite Dolley would have had a hard time dismantling the towering work. A slave, aged fifteen at the time, later clouded the issue further, when he let it drop that while Mrs. Madison was concerned about the painting, she was more worried about the family silver. But even with all that, history records that she kept her wits somewhat better than her husband James, who, to be fair, never claimed to be George Patton.

In the Revolution, Madison had been commissioned a militia colonel, although he was too sickly to serve. As the British approached Washington, he and his cabinet members had, after retrieving the missing spyglass, gamely ridden into battle, but as Howe wrote, he was "not able to control his horse, much less his army." Like the militia, the president and his cabinet scattered far and wide at the first sight of the gleaming enemy sabers, an event that clearly tickled Gleig, who noted that the president "discover[ed] that his presence was more wanted in the Senate than in the field." To illustrate how fast the situation was deteriorating, Madison had time to dispatch two scribbled notes to his wife, the first which essentially said remain calm all is well, the second of which instructed his loved ones to run for their lives.

The inglorious episode was brutally satirized a couple of days later in a poem called "The Bladensburg Races," depicting the skittishness of Madison and Monroe in the field, particularly as it related to the president's warhorse, which apparently spooked at the sound of a military bugle call:

And Winder do not fire your guns,
Or let your trumpet play,
Till we are out of sight—Forsooth,
My horse will run away.

So too did cartoonists have a grand time lampooning the absentee president. The president was gone, the cabinet was gone, and Congress, as usual, was on vacation. As there was no means of direct communication, Dolley Madison might have been at that point the closest thing the capital had to a leader. After securing what government valuables she could, Dolley and members of the staff fled to Virginia, where one last indignity remained; she was denied respite at a farmhouse by a woman who was irked that her husband had been called up for service in the militia. In 1815, even being the wife of a Founding Father was no guarantee of respect, a good reminder that those men whom today are viewed as borderline gods were likely as not to be seen by some as coarse politicians in their day. And when disaster struck, it was the president himself who got the blame.

The field won, the British officers pushed their reserves who had not been needed in battle to lead the way into Washington. Ross had no thought of occupying the capital, but he did mean to do damage. There was one last chance at accommodation, but this vaporized when some hothead in a nearby residence shot the horse out from under an American officer who was seeking terms under a white flag of truce. The British rousted the occupants, ran them through with their swords, set the house afire, and from there it was Katy bar the door.

Hell-bent, they stormed the city, setting fire to the federal office buildings, the national archives, federal printing offices, and the Capitol building, which proved a troublesome chore due to its stone construction. Finally, they heaped all the desks and chairs into a pile, which burned adequately enough to destroy the handsome building, along the congressional library. (Thomas Jefferson later bailed himself out of debt by selling his own library to Congress as a replacement.)

It seemed as if the British knew exactly where to go, despite being in unfamiliar surroundings. They darted from one federal building to another as easily as if they had hired a twenty-first-century tour guide, fueling suspicions that some traitors must have been in the mix to help the Redcoats along. Into the evening and early-morning hours they hit the Potomac dockyards, burning barracks, destroying ships, and blowing up powder magazines. They were not targeting private residences, but it said something about the shacks and shanties of greater Washington at the time that a number of houses collapsed from the concussion of exploding stores of gunpowder.

Gleig, for his part, felt his own troops went too far by burning nonmilitary establishments, although in the end he blamed the Americans for not putting up a better defense. "The capture of Washington was more owing to the blindness of the Americans themselves than to any cause," he wrote. "From the beginning to the end of the affair they acted in no one instance like prudent or sagacious people."

. Not everyone had fled in advance, and the Scottish soldier said the remaining citizens regretted their error in judgment: "I need scarcely observe that the consternation of the inhabitants was complete, and that to them this was a night of terror. So confident had they been of the success of their troops that few of them had dreamt of quitting their houses or abandoning the city, nor was it till the fugitives from the battle began to rush in, filling every place as they came with dismay that the President himself thought of providing for his safety" above that of the people.

Official Washington had been caught off guard as well. Before events on the battlefield had gone so horribly wrong, a sumptuous dinner had been planned for forty guests at the White House in anticipation of a great victory. Cut-glass decanters on the sideboards were filed with various wines, the table was set with silver cutlery, and plates were warming by the fireplace. In the kitchen, pots and saucepans bubbled with delicious side dishes and great roasts of beef and mutton sizzled on turning spits. When the British arrived, the only thing missing was any trace of human occupation.

A boisterous victory feast was indeed held in the presidential palace that evening, although the guest list was not as anticipated. It was not a refined gathering of officers and bureaucrats, but rough, dirty, and famished soldiers who drained the decanters and gorged on the meat. Then, satisfied, they vacated the dining room and set the White House afire.

As the British reserves were bringing ruin to Washington's government buildings, the soldiers who had done battle settled in outside of the city for the night to rest and recuperate. They watched and listened with interest as the night sky reddened with flames and the ground shook with exploding powder magazines and collapsing roofs. But with the new day, however, the fire on the ground was matched by fire on high, and the rumble and crash of thunder joined the cacophony of destruction occurring in the city. The heat wave had played havoc not just with the soldiers, but with the upper atmosphere, and now a storm of epic proportions was approaching.

For the residents of Washington, the simultaneous arrival of the British and Mother Nature had to be terrifying. In the early nineteenth century, superstition still ruled the day, and all kinds of meaning would have been read into the impending storm. If the residents hadn't been inclined to flee before, they were now. Carriages, people, wagons, and horses milled about the streets, stymied by Madison's orders to dismantle the sole bridge across the Potomac River. The president himself had escaped to the Quaker settlement of Brookeville, which became cynically known as "the American capital for a day." All told, James Madison, author of our Constitution, was not a popular man that August.

The British design was to destroy only government buildings, but as the flames grew higher, private residences were at risk as well. Washington was at this point in its history a town of scattered buildings and unfinished roads. There would be no great house-to-house conflagration of the type that ripped through London or Chicago. But embers floating on the wind and showers of sparks from multiple explosions seemed certain to set the downtown commercial and residential districts ablaze as well. But with the fires at their height, the skies opened up and a deluge doused the flames before they could spread beyond their intended targets. Along with the rains came a windstorm that few had seen the likes of before.

According to the book *Washington Weather*, "the tornado tore through the center of Washington and directly into the British occupation. Buildings were lifted off their foundations and dashed to bits. Other buildings were blown down or lost their roofs." The air was a bizarre, swirling stew of leaves, twigs, papers, and feathers from beds that had been sucked from homes and shredded.

For this, it became known as "The Storm that Saved Washington," although there is some discussion over whom the bad weather helped more. Before the locals could crow about Providence being on their side, the storm system delivered a second punch that arguably favored the invaders. *Washington Weather* records an exchange between a British officer and a testy townswoman: "Great God, Madam!" the officer said. "Is this the kind of storm to which you are accustomed in this infernal country?" The lady answered, "No, Sir, this is a special interposition of Providence to drive our enemies from our city." The admiral replied, "Not so, Madam. It is rather to aid your enemies in the destruction of your city."

In truth, it did both. An obviously impressed Gleig described the storm this way: "Of the prodigious force of the wind it is impossible for one who was not an eye witness to its effects to form a conception. Roofs of houses were torn off by it and whirled into the air like sheets of paper whilst the rain which accompanied it resembled the rushing of a mighty cataract rather than the dropping of a shower. The darkness was as great as if the sun had long set and the last remains of twilight had come on occasionally relieved by flashes of vivid lightning streaming through it, which together with the noise of the wind and the thunder, the crash of falling buildings and the tearing of roofs as they were stript from the walls, produced the most appalling effect I ever have and probably ever shall witness."

Based on eyewitness accounts, the National Weather Service classifies the storm that saved Washington as a tornado. The winds were strong enough to flip cannons on their backs, and if the British hadn't had enough of the crazy Americans and their crazy country by this time, the crazy weather sealed it. Adding to their conviction was the appearance, just prior to the tornado, of a larger American force on the horizon, but by this time the British didn't need to be told twice. They went on to attack Baltimore two weeks later, where they were rebuffed, and they simultaneously suffered a stunning setback on Lake

Champlain in the Battle of Plattsburgh Bay. In the end, this was a war no one wanted. A peace was drawn up leaving everything mostly the same as it had been before the war.

In September, Madison called Congress back into session, and working in temporary, uncomfortable quarters, among their first orders of business was consideration of a bill to move the capital to some more commodious city, namely Philadelphia. But Washington investors—understanding that their properties would have no earthly value without the seat of government to lean on, raised $25,000 for a temporary capitol, and Congress voted 83–74 to stay put.

CHAPTER 3

Presidential Ambition Ends
in Catastrophe

William Henry Harrison lived a rich and full life, but he is best known for dying. The fact of his death, just thirty days after assuming the US presidency is more popularly recognizable today than, say, the expansionist policies of James K. Polk.

Multiple generations of mothers also employ the circumstances surrounding the president's death as anecdotal, if erroneous, reinforcement for their plaintive entreaties to their children to wear a coat. Inaugurated on a cold wet March day, and riding hatless on a horse instead of bundled up in a carriage, the old Indian fighter sought to prove his vitality by speaking in the cold rain for two hours, before attending a series of inaugural balls late into the night.

While not directly responsible for the pneumonia he would contract in another three weeks, the day certainly left him exhausted, as did the custom in those days of a nonstop parade to the president's personal office of callers seeking favors and appointments.

Harrison's death left the presidency to Vice President John Tyler, who felt more strongly about his ascendancy than did the written Constitution itself, which only mentioned in passing that the in the event of the Top Dog's demise, the duties (but not necessarily the title) of the president should "devolve" to the VP. Tyler took the word "devolve" and ran with it, almost immediately taking the oath of office before anyone could come up with a better idea. Nominally a Whig (a party that would somewhat resemble a more liberal Chamber of Commerce), Tyler almost immediately alienated his own party by vetoing bills he believed to run contrary to the Constitution. Given his shaky claim to the executive office and his thirst for executive overreach, like many modern-day pols, Tyler strictly adhered to the Constitution—but only when convenient. His rapidly accumulating enemies responded by mockingly christening him with the nickname "His Accidency."

By then it was apparent that it was all coming apart for the Whigs who, whatever their attributes, were one of the most duplicitous political parties in America, which is obviously saying a lot. It's been argued that they were in part done in by the telegraph, which ended their habit of telling disparate regions of the country what they wanted to hear, confident that the people had no way of knowing that members of the same party had promised another region something else entirely.

The Whigs were substantively led by Henry Clay of Kentucky, and had used the popular Harrison and the geographically expedient Tyler, a Virginian, to defeat incumbent President Martin Van Buren, a Jacksonian Democrat who had the misfortune of presiding over the Panic of 1837. But even though Harrison wasn't around long, he was around long enough to get across the point through his cabinet picks that he had used the Whigs as much as they had used him. But where Harrison differed with Clay mostly on matters of personnel for the cabinet, Tyler differed with Clay on virtually everything.

Tyler has been hailed as a man of principles, but too often those principles metastasized as crabby tirades against various government policies—even policies he supported—if he felt they were being achieved without constitutional purity. His obsession with the means put him squarely at odds with the ends-focused Whigs, even on those rare occasions where they agreed. Tyler showed no deference to the party that had selected him for its ticket, vetoing any and all Whig legislation he felt extended beyond the Constitution's shadow. This, to the Whigs, was a strange way of saying thanks.

When Tyler vetoed the second national banking act to cross his desk, the Whigs hatched a plan that was typically Whiggish in its bizarre orchestration. One by one, with the sole exception of Secretary of State Daniel Webster, the Whig members of Tyler's cabinet walked into His Accidency's office and submitted their resignation, the idea being that Tyler would be so embarrassed/ashamed/horrified that he himself would resign.

As Will Rodgers once said of Communism, it was a good idea, but it didn't work. Not only did Tyler remain, he took publicly pegged Clay as his sworn enemy, to which Clay's Whigs responded by tossing Tyler out of the party altogether and bombarding the president with death threats and demonstrations. So poisoned was the well, that Congress even refused to appropriate money to maintain the White House.

To the modern student of politics, the elevated level of bickering at the time over policy and finance, seem both anachronistic and hauntingly familiar. Today, the federal government probably spends $11 million on toothpicks, but in 1841 this was the sum total of the federal deficit. Still, it was a troublesome point as the economy continued to struggle from a panic in 1837, and patchwork fixes were failing to slow the red ink. Before the days of the income tax, only two sources of revenue offered practical solutions: tariffs and proceeds from the sale of federal lands. The Whigs favored the former, Tyler the latter, and the whole issue blew up in a conflagration that makes the rift over Obamacare seem like a disagreement over picking up the check at Applebee's. Twice the Whigs tried to get a revenue package into law and twice Tyler vetoed it. At this point in America's history, the president could not veto a bill simply because he disagreed with it; a veto was only appropriate if the president thought the law to be unconstitutional. However, the Whigs sensed an opportunity, and for the first time, Congress launched an impeachment investigation against a sitting president. Henry Clay felt Tyler's impeachment was "inevitable," and it might have been had the Whigs not lost control of the House in the 1842 elections.

The hatred between the executive and the legislature played out in a number of childish ways that, again, sound dismally familiar to the modern ear. Congress refused to approve

Tyler's cabinet appointments, another first in US history. The rejection of his nominees regardless of their qualifications predictably steamed the president, who took to renominating the same individual immediately after Congress had voted the nomination down. Tyler's nomination for Treasury, Caleb Cushing, had the dubious honor of being voted down three times in the same day. Tyler had no more luck filling two vacancies on the Supreme Court, as the Whigs felt they could stonewall long enough that the vacancies would be filled by the next president, who they hoped would be Henry Clay. Congress rejected Edward King (twice), Reuben Walworth (three times), John Spencer and John Read, once each. Even more ground was broken in 1845 when Congress, for the first time, overrode a presidential veto.

Tyler meanwhile demonstrated his fealty to the Constitution by trying to figure out how to cut the legislature out of the governing process altogether, and his eyes finally came to rest on foreign affairs, where the executive could operate unilaterally. Determined that we today should remember the name "Tyler" with the same reverence and awe with which we remember Washington and Jefferson, Tyler sought a dramatic, high-octane play that would seal his legacy for all time. He found it, or so he thought, in the Republic of Texas, then a sprawling territory that had won independence from Mexico and included a great swath of what is now the American Southwest. If he could bring Texas into the fold, he might be remembered the same way Jefferson had been applauded for his Louisiana Purchase.

But as with the case with just about everything at the time, the Texas matter was seen through the lens of slavery;

abolitionists were not about to allow another slave state (and more importantly, two more pro-slave senators) to enter the union, so the initiative stalled, almost before it commenced. For the time being, President John Tyler would have to be content with a series of useful but relatively minor treaties that focused on foreign trade and the future annexation of the Hawaiian Islands.

Meantime, Tyler hoped the emotion around the Texas issue would die down, which it didn't. There is historical dispute over Tyler's personal view of slavery (then, as now, people were complex; slave owners were not universally pro-slavery, just as abolitionists did not necessarily view black people as their equals, or at least not as people they would be comfortable having a beer with). However, it seems safe to say the president was pro-slavery, but not in the Deep South firebrand way.

And as it turned out, Tyler the Constitutional ideologue had a practical streak running through him after all. He wanted to annex Texas and he was ready to deal. This wasn't entirely a matter of the Virginian's legacy, it was also a matter of political survival. The Whigs had of course booted out Tyler on his ear, and no other party seemed interested in investing in what was seen as damaged goods. Tyler's reelection depended on some bold stroke that would win public acclaim.

This touched off a curious dance that reached from Texas to Great Britain to the Pacific Northwest, and involved several other men of ambition that, together, led to, as the *New York Herald* would later put it, "one of the most horrible and heart-rending catastrophes that ever took place in this or any other country." It all began, as these things do, with a turf battle.

Schoolchildren who spend too much time studying maps no doubt notice that the State of Minnesota has an interesting lump on its head, a peg of land that protrudes into Canada; it's the only part of the contiguous United States to reach above the 49th parallel, and gives the Gopher State claim to being the northernmost of the lower forty-eight. But it was an accident. The Treaty of Paris that ended the Revolution called for a boundary between British and American territories based on the assumption that the Mississippi River ran north to the present-day Canadian border, which it doesn't. The Treaty of 1818 between Britain and the United States cleaned up this detail, or tried to, except that it left Minnesota with an extra six hundred square miles of land above the 49th parallel that today is home to about 150 people.

Mapmakers knew this was not ideal, but at this point they just said forget it, because the 1818 treaty had larger concerns, including whether the Americans or the British had right to the Oregon Territory (today much of the American Northwest). In an epic display of kicking the can down the road, the diplomats agreed that both countries could control the territory, claiming land and freely traveling as they saw fit. This was only fifteen years after the Lewis and Clark expedition after all, so it wasn't as if developers on either side were clamoring to build condos.

Except in the early 1840s, John Tyler and his Secretary of State Abel Upshur were beginning to see a practical use for the territory—not so much for the land itself, but as a bargaining chip. Upshur had taken over the position Secretary of State from Daniel Webster, before which he had been Tyler's Secretary of the Navy, where he had been instrumental in transforming a sleepy, neglected agency into a force actually capable of putting up a fight. As many times as the British had clobbered the Americans on the high seas, there had been disturbingly little emphasis in Washington on catching up. President Martin Van Buren—whose greatest political achievement was extinguishing a growing catfight among the wives of President Andrew Jackson's cabinet members—didn't even see why a navy was necessary.

Upshur organized an efficient naval bureaucracy that replaced a three-man commission that was somehow supposed to oversee all the Navy's business from commissioning ships to filling out purchase orders for rope. But the greatest mountain Upshur had to scale was convincing the nation's old salts to make the switch from sail to steam. In the nineteenth century, military bureaucracy was often slow to warm to new technology; Union officers in the Civil War, for example, were unimpressed with the repeating rifle because they feared the troops would blow through too much ammunition. And, while commercial steamships had been operating successfully for two decades, many crusty old naval officers felt that steamers were ugly, noisy, dirty, and lacked the grace of the elegant sailing ships. Never mind that a steamship could outrun and outmaneuver the fastest sailing vessels—naval officers were a remarkably romantic bunch.

Back in Texas, Sam Houston, who had whipped the Mexican army at San Jacinto in precisely eighteen minutes to win independence, was finding himself to be the most popular politician in the western world. Not only was he courted by Tyler and Upshur, he was courted by the British who were either genuinely interested in acquiring Texas or just intent on making trouble for Washington by undermining the institution of slavery in Texas and beyond. Houston was canny enough to play both sides. The only man to be governor of two states (Tennessee and Texas), Houston was also the only Southern governor who opposed secession on the eve of the Civil War—a position for which the past and future Texas hero was unceremoniously removed from office.

Houston had no intention of throwing his lot in with the British, but in his view Washington didn't need to know that because he hoped rumors of British interest would light a fire under Tyler and Upshur to grant Texas statehood. Not that they needed much incentive in that regard, having tied their personal interests to the project. But there was still the slave state problem, which was where the Oregon Territory came in. Not a lot of cotton was being grown in Oregon, which Tyler felt that he could bring in as a free state to counterbalance the slave state of Texas. But British entanglement in Oregon under the Treaty of 1818 was still a problem, and soon a new matter came to light that changed the attitude of Northerner and Southerner alike. Mistrust over British intentions in Texas came to a full boil when it was leaked that the Brits were trying to broker an understanding between Mexico and Texas that could potentially lead to the Republic becoming an autonomous Mexican state.

Slavery in Mexico had been abolished in 1829 and it was too easy to imagine what would happen to American slavery if the Texas slave market dried up. At least that was the Southern fear. Northerners still needed to be won over to the cause of Texas statehood, and that came through the everlasting hope of Manifest Destiny and the fear that successful British initiatives to free the slaves would ultimately attract blacks into their own personal neighborhoods (nineteenth-century NIMBY, as it were). The latter notion was perpetuated by a Mississippi US senator named Robert J. Walker, who believed that without the steady guidance of their white masters, slaves would inevitably go insane. Freed slaves, Walker told the nervous North, would fan out across the nation to the point that "the poorhouse and the jail, the asylums of the deaf and dumb, the blind, the idiot and insane, would be filled to overflowing."

The way to prevent this cataclysm, of course, was by annexing Texas, which would eventually act as a "slave valve." Even without the Civil War, the institution of slavery was becoming top-heavy, as visionaries predicted that the jobs performed by slaves would in the not-too-distant future be done by machines. And then what? Where would the slaves go, and what would they do? Texas might disperse the slave population, farming them out to points in Central and South America and the Carribean where slavery was still permitted. Without the slaves technically being freed, the population would nevertheless leak away and the nation could just wash its hands of the whole thing. Southerners wouldn't have to worry about losing their investments and Northerners wouldn't have to worry about freedmen moving in next-door. But as annexation gained momentum, there was still one big problem: Mexico. Any attempt to interfere with Texas might trigger a military reaction from Mexicans sympathetic to Santa Anna, who was still pretty sore about losing Texas in the first place.

To keep Mexico from getting any bright ideas, Tyler and Upshur needed to put on a display of military strength, and the right person to facilitate that was a full-of-himself naval commander who happened to share Upshur's ideas about modernizing America's navy. Commodore Robert F. Stockton was equal parts talent and ego. A native of New Jersey whose father had served in the US Senate and whose grandfather had signed the Declaration of Independence, Stockton entered the Navy as a midshipman in 1811 at the age of sixteen, and compiled an impressive resume fighting the British in the War of 1812 and the Barbary pirates and capturing a number of ships illegally involved in the slave trade. But it was also true that those who worked with Stockton found that small doses of his company were quite sufficient, and by the 1820s it was clear that the naval brass wanted him to take his talents elsewhere.

Which he did, succeeding in business and making a fortune to add to the fortune he had inherited. He was quite generous with his money, using it to lavishly wine and dine anyone he thought capable of furthering his career, up to and including the president of the United States. But his belief in the need for a fleet of modern warships (commanded, of course, by he himself) was sincere, so it was no real surprise when at the behest of the Tyler administration he was back in the Navy in 1841 charged with introducing the latest technology to the American fleet. With one eye on Britain and one on Mexico, Upshur and Stockton had one priority: They wanted the fastest ship carrying the biggest guns.

This dream materialized in a craft christened the USS *Princeton*, Stockton humbly naming it after his hometown. The steamer's drivetrain was designed by the brilliant John Ericsson, a Swede who won greater fame by building the USS *Monitor*, the Union's ironclad that battled the CSS *Virginia* to a draw in the first battle between two ironclads two decades later. Built in the shipyards of Philadelphia, *Princeton* was not a particularly large ship at a length of 164 feet, but she had some unique advantages, most notably that she was powered not by the typical paddlewheel, but by a screw propeller (for redundancy, she was also outfitted as a fully rigged sailing ship). Part of the reason the Navy was reluctant to give up on sailing ships was that the bulk of a sidewheeler's powertrain was above deck, where it could easily be disabled by one well-placed cannonball. The underwater propulsion system was largely invulnerable to gunfire. The ship's boilers were fueled by cleaner-burning anthracite coal, which mitigated another steamship disadvantage, the towering plume of smoke that would give away a ship's location.

But coup de grace was two of the biggest naval guns known to man, each capable of hurling a 225-pound ball a distance of five miles. One had been designed in part by Ericsson, who had it made at the Mercey Iron Works in Liverpool and shipped to American shores. Constructed out of wrought iron instead of cast iron, it was something of an experiment. Cannon had typically been cast, the molten metal poured into a mold. Wrought iron had less carbon and more impurities, and was therefore more malleable. Once iron was cast, that was it; it would shatter instead of bend. Wrought or "worked" iron, however could be heated and manipulated. Stockton sensed this might be an advantage, and when the big new cannon arrived it was buried in the sand and fired. It held. So the gun was mounted onto a carriage and fired again. On this attempt, smoke wafted from a fissure in the barrel, and when water was used to clean the gun barrel it leaked right out.

Oddly, this was good news. With a similar flaw in a brittle cast-iron gun, the barrel would have blown apart. Stockton was so impressed, he shored up the breech by wrapping it with a couple of heavy iron bands, and, after extensive and successful testing, he ordered up a second gun based on the first—except, Stockton being Stockton, he made sure it would be noticeably bigger than Ericsson's. It was, after all, his call, seeing as how he was paying for it—and much of the ship itself—out of his own pocket (compared to the Congress of 1844, today's version is a fountain of generosity).

Stockton's weapon weighed in at an astounding thirteen and a half tons, and since it was larger than the Mercey gun and made from superior American ore, a subsequent board of inquiry found no reason to believe Stockton had not acted prudently. Unmentioned was the fact that its construction had been rushed to accommodate the commodore's agenda. Stockton named it the Peacemaker, while Ericsson's was christened the Oregon: Oregon as a shot over the British bow, and Peacemaker as a reminder to the Mexicans not to start anything they couldn't finish.

Stockton reveled in his new ship, sailing and steaming along the Eastern Seaboard to New York, where he raced the *Great Western*, a commercial trans-Atlantic, side-wheel steamer thought to be the fastest boat on the seas. Belching clouds of inky smoke and her paddlewheel thrashing away like a cat in a pail of ice water, the *Great Western* was lapped by the clean and quiet *Princeton*. Her prowess established, *Princeton* was ready for prime time.

After a couple of warm-up runs on the Potomac, Stockton sent out exclusive invitations for a glorious river cruise, featuring sumptuous food, fine wine, and fireworks in the form of thunderous reports of the massive Peacemaker. The guest list for the February 28 demonstration included the president and his cabinet, a Mexican emissary, and a seventy-five-year-old Dolley Madison. It also included a saucy debutante from Long Island named Julia Gardiner who had taken Washington by storm, winning the hearts of men in low places and high, men in their teens and men three times her age. Among her suitors were Stockton's own son, a Supreme Court justice—and President John Tyler himself. Julia was accompanying her wealthy father David whom she adored, and her presence on the steamer that day would change history.

For February, it was an excellent day—clear as a bell and temperate. "The day was surprisingly beautiful," according to one dispatch. "The sun rose clear and bright and the town in the early morning presented a gay and busy scene. Nearly all the carriages were engaged, and freighted with the loveliness, beauty and grace of the city." Their passengers boarded a ferry to cross the Potomac, stopping at the Navy Yard to take onboard a military band. When the *Princeton* hove into view, her elegant curves rising from the water's surface and colorful flags of every nation flying above the decks, a mighty cheer arose from the ferry and the band struck up "Hail Columbia." Marines presented arms, and the women were urged to go below so as not to have their delicate senses offended by the acrid smoke from the twenty-one-gun salute. There was no small amount of amusement in the crowd when the women told the sailors to kiss their yardarms, this was a scene they weren't going to miss. As the crowd of up to four hundred guests strolled across the gangplank of a river ferry onto *Princeton's* hurricane deck, it was hard to overstate the importance the upcoming twenty-five or so miles, upon which a number of important men hoped to build not just their careers, but their legacies. Secretary of State Upshur had brilliantly played his hand on the issue of Texas annexation, and assumed Congress would fall dutifully into line within the coming days. Captain Stockton and Thomas Gilmer, secretary of the Navy, believed that Americans forevermore would look back on this as the watershed day, a sign that the fleet had turned the corner from a collection of sorry old tubs toward becoming a world superpower. The British and Mexicans too were keenly interested to see whether the warship would live up to its billing as a fast, stealthy killing machine or if this were just another case of groundless and tiresome bragging by the Americans. And of course, this was Tyler's last best chance to win a second term. Unpopular with the partisan establishment, Tyler had taken his case directly to the people and the pubic had yet to meet a saber rattler it didn't like.

Princeton steamed smartly down the Potomac, slicing neatly through the blue water, her sharp prow sending up white spray to the delight of the passengers hearty enough to populate the open deck above. For most, however, this was a social, not a military, exercise—a chance to see and be seen and swill the expensive champagne that the captain had thoughtfully provided. Stockton had made sure that the guest list was evenly divided between men and women, and the papers reported "great hilarity" consumed those fortunate enough to receive an invitation.

But as the river widened below Fort Washington, it was time for the moment that all comers, regardless of motivation, had been waiting for. The call went out that the Peacemaker was about to show off its awesome power. Everyone was called to the forecastle, a raised deck at the stern of the ship, as sailors dumped more than thirty pounds of powder into the breech and rammed home a ball a foot in diameter. Much as they braced themselves, the crowd could in no way prepare for the thunderous report of the big gun, as it sent its ordnance back upstream. Men jumped, women screamed, and then they all had a good laugh at their own skittishness. Rather than sending the ball high and out of sight, gunners launched it parallel to the river, astonishing viewers who watched the big ball of iron skip lightly a half dozen times along the water like a flat stone on a farm pond before disappearing into the Potomac.

As the guests began to dine in shifts, once more the Peacemaker mesmerized the crowd, interspaced with lively music and fine food. Stockton was literally the toast of the excursion, as glasses were lifted in his honor at the successful demonstration. At one point, Upshur grabbed a bottle for a toast, and finding it empty, wisecracked that he couldn't give a proper toast with a dead soldier, to which Stockton assured him, to the guffaws of the crowd, that there were plenty of live soldiers to take its place. The pride and sense of importance the captain felt—and had in fact earned, seeing as how he had recognized the technology and paid for construction—at that moment had to have been immense. Of that there can be little doubt.

What happened next is not as clear. *Princeton* had come to the end of her voyage south and had turned for her return trip to Alexandria. As she was pulling abreast of Mount Vernon, it was suggested, perhaps by Gilmer, that the gun be fired in honor of George Washington. Stockton partisans said the captain, fearing the gun might be overheated, was reluctant and had to be talked into it. Others say he was more than happy to show off his weapon once again. At least some of the ladies, reckoning that you've seen one canon shot you've seen them all, chose to remain below, picking away at their sumptuous lunch. But the men were keen to see another gunshot, and besides, it would be bad form to snub the founder of the country's memory. The president's cabinet members went topside. Tyler was in this group, but was delayed at the last minute—some say a dignitary wanted a word, and some say he wanted to hear a favored song. But the more romantic view is that he stayed below out of fear that the apple of his eye, Julia Gardiner, might take up with one of her many other suitors in his absence. The *New York Herald* reported in fact that "President Tyler was [on board] also, but had attended the ladies to dinner before the third discharge."

When Tyler's two cabinet members took their place with other VIPs in the place of honor on the port side of the Peacemaker, they looked around for their president—his personal slave and valet Armistead was there, apparently waiting for him. Upshur and Gilmer would have likely chatted with Julia's father David as the sailors prepared the gun, perhaps about the family's recent tour of Europe, something of a self-imposed exile from the Long Island gossip mills after the fun-loving Julia had imprudently posed for a handbill advertising a clothing shop popular among the commoners. Or they might have talked about the progress of the new Navy with the department's chief of construction Beverly Kennon, or chatted up the dapper Marylander Virgil Maxcy about his extensive holdings in slaves and land. (Maxcy, fifty-eight, was an accomplished attorney and an envoy to Belgium, but historians have spent more time parsing a letter he wrote to a male friend which includes the line, "I think I have hold of your doodle when in reality I have hold of the bedpost." In the 1800s it was quite common for heterosexual men to sleep in the same bed and maybe even spoon a bit, but Maxcy's comment seemed to imply something more, leading scholars to wonder if the husband and father was perhaps a closeted gay—and more lowbrow readers to wonder whether it was an extra-skinny bedpost or one whale of a doodle.)

As *Princeton* came abreast of Mount Vernon, with the sun sinking low in the southwest, the ceremonial firing could no longer wait and a charge was put to the big gun. Those to the right and rear of Peacemaker didn't at first realize anything was wrong. The ear-splitting report and thick belch of acrid smoke were a bit more intense perhaps, but otherwise mostly par for the course. It was only as the smoke wafted away that onlookers beheld the terrible scene before them. As reported by the *New York Herald*, "The gun was fired. The explosion was followed, before the smoke cleared away so as to observe its effects by shrieks of wo[e] which announced the dire calamity. The gun had burst at a point three or four feet from the breech and scattered death and desolation around." Navel gunners staggered blindly around the deck; some were driven to their knees or knocked fully unconscious by the concussive force of the Peacemaker blowing apart. Captain Stockton, who had been standing to the right-rear of the gun with his boot jauntily resting on the carriage, hit the deck with a piece of shrapnel through the foot, but quickly bounced back up to survey the scene. The powder flash had incinerated his prized hair and whiskers, and for weeks after the accident the vain captain was reluctant to be seen in public.

Those who had seen Stockton's blackened face assumed he must be dead, or near so, an error that was reported in many of the next day's papers. In reality, his wounds were largely superficial. But it was on the left-hand side of the cannon that the real horror presented itself. Shocked guests discovered a pile of mutilated corpses where just a few seconds before some of the nation's most important men had stood. The newspapers spared no effort in inventorying the exact number of limbs and bowels blown asunder on each of the unfortunate victims. Few of these reports agreed, but it hardly mattered. Legs and arms were scattered around the deck as the left side of the massive cannon sent shards, some weighing up to a ton, of hot iron ripping through the helpless onlookers at point-blank range.

Killed were Secretary of State Upshur, Secretary of the Navy Gilmore, Commodore Kennon, Virgil Maxcy, David Gardiner, and Armistead. It took two men to lift a piece of iron off the chest of Upshur, whose clothes had blown from his body with the force of the explosion. Also dying instantly was Maxcy, who lost both arms and a leg, "the pieces of flesh hanging to the mutilated limbs cold and bloodless in a manner truly frightful," an eyewitness helpfully reported. The rest lingered no more than half an hour, without regaining consciousness.

After being briefly treated, Stockton limped back to the forecastle and resumed command over a scene of increasing despair. Gardiner's two daughters were inconsolable at the news, while Gilmer's wife seemed unable to process what had just happened. An eyewitness thought *Hamlet*'s Ophelia was an apt comparison: "There she sat on deck, with hair disheveled, pale as death, struggling with her feelings, and with the dignity of a woman. Her lips quivering, her eyes fixed and upturned, without a tear, only the corners a little moist, soliloquizing, Oh! Certainly not! Who would dare injure him?"

It would be Tyler himself who cared for the swooning Julia. The young woman lost a father but effectively gained a husband that day, as within months she had accepted Tyler's standing proposal of marriage, something she showed no interest in before. Thirty years her senior (Tyler was ten years older than his disapproving mother-in-law, and Julia would inherit disapproving stepchildren older than she), Tyler was ridiculed as a "foolish old jackass" and Julia was pitied as a girl in desperate need of a father figure. Whatever others thought, they were happy and Julia, not without some growing pains, became a respectable First Lady in her husband's final months in office. No shrinking violet she, Julia insisted that the band play "Hail to the Chief" when her betrothed entered the room, a tradition that has lasted to this day.

Although they numbered half of the passengers present on board, no women were among the casualties. Many had remained below-deck, but those who came to watch, due to their height, either stood on other guns to see, or sat on a specially built viewing platform. There were other near misses reported. Tyler's son was on board as well, but as he scampered up the stairs a buzzed chum fortuitously grabbed him by the scruff of the neck and dragged him back below for another drink. Secretary of War William Wilkins was standing with the other cabinet members prior to the explosion before he, in a bit of self-deprecating humor, quipped that he was perhaps the only secretary of war who did not like the sound of gunfire. He went below and saved himself.

The explosion occurred at about four in the afternoon, and news reached Washington three hours later and stunned the nation's capital. Even the *Whig Standard*, no fan of the Tyler administration, was aghast: "The gloom that now pervades our city is deep and melancholy in the extreme." It was the worst peacetime disaster the capital had known. A funeral procession a mile long passed through its streets. Yet even this was not without incident, as the horses pulling Tyler's carriage spooked and he and his son were taken on a madcap dash through the crowd until a black man whose identity was never known managed to save the president, who for the second time in a week had come within an inch of his life.

But with the explosion of the Peacemaker, John Tyler's political career was beyond saving. In a disaster not quite as hideous as the *Princeton's*, but close, Tyler appointed the passionate (passionate to his friends, unhinged to his enemies) John C. Calhoun to replace Upshur Secretary of State, and the fire-eating South Carolinian temporarily ran the prospects of Texas annexation clean off the rails. It had taken every ounce of diplomacy in Upshur's body to sell Congress on the notion that Texas statehood was a benefit to the nation as a whole and had nothing to do with slavery. But to Calhoun, everything was about slavery, and he wanted everyone to know it. Worse, when he discovered an unanswered letter to Upshur from a British minister assuring the late secretary that the British had no intention of interfering in America's Texas ambitions—but casually mentioning that they still believed slavery to be a moral issue worth agitating against—Calhoun went ballistic. With the fury of a 3 a.m. tweet, he fired off a thunderous response that included a reference to the 1840 Census, which he argued proved that slaves who were freed from their bonds more often than not went insane. When confronted with proof that the Census data proved no such thing, Calhoun shrugged, and with an explanation that would have been toasted by fans of alternative facts everywhere, insisted that the inaccuracies in his numbers were irrelevant because the Census made other mistakes too, so it all balanced out.

Had he lived, Upshur might have been remembered as Jefferson and Seward were for their land acquisitions. As it is, among his few namesakes is a rural county in West Virginia. Tyler did indeed sign Texas annexation into law in the waning days of his presidency, but only after he was an unthreatening lame duck, and only after engaging an early variation of the "nuclear option," in which he abandoned the standard treaty approach that would have required a two-thirds Senate majority and presenting it as a resolution that required only a simple majority. Texas was annexed in February 1845, a year after the *Princeton* disaster, and it became a state that December. Five months later, the United States and Mexico were at war— rather than being intimidated by the *Princeton's* star-crossed demonstration, the Mexicans had taken it as a sign that the Americans' military technology was nowhere near as advanced as it had been advertised.

Almost from the time the smoke cleared following the explosion, Captain Stockton worked almost frantically to absolve himself of any responsibility. Some of the earliest reports out of Washington included references to the captain's supposed reluctance to fire the gun a third time, and stressed that it was an accident pure and simple. Tyler quickly jumped to Stockton's defense, saying that the disaster was just one of those things that no one could have prevented. So too did the sympathetic Commission on Naval Affairs that almost sounded as if the nation should be grateful to Stockton for the explosion. After a somewhat shallow investigation, it concluded that "not only was every precaution taken which skill, regulated by prudence, and animated by the loftiest motives, could devise to guard against accident," but that the captain and crew must have believed it to be safe since they obviously felt comfortable to stand next to the Peacemaker when it was fired. This was a bit like saying that Captain Edward J. Smith never would have boarded the *Titanic* if he thought he was going to steer it into an iceberg, but the public seemed satisfied.

More circumspect was the more professional and less political Franklin Institute, whose Committee on Science and the Arts conducted its own inquiry, as did the House Committee on Naval Affairs. Both implicated Stockton indirectly for rushing the process and failing to solicit second opinions (a point Stockton hotly denied). The impurities, or slag, that gave the wrought iron its elastic qualities had to be handled properly in order to have the desired result. It created air pockets that had to be worked out of the metal, and foundries at that time didn't have hammers big enough to do the job on so massive a weapon. And while it was perhaps admirable that Stockton himself paid for the ship, this provided for no oversight. There was no check on Stockton's judgment. This was particularly apparent when the Swedish inventor Ericsson (whom Stockton had dumped, some say, out of professional jealousy) declined to testify because, he noted sourly, the time to solicit his expertise would have been before the explosion.

Stockton continued to serve and to serve well during the Mexican-American War. But because of the *Princeton* disaster he would not be known as the man who transformed the American Navy. In fact, the setback only petrified the old salts' prejudices against steam, propellers, and weapons of mass destruction.

The ship itself met an ignoble end. So much attention had been given to her arms and power train that somehow her wooden underpinnings were neglected, and the ship rotted from within. A scant six years after her commissioning, she was broken apart for scrap.

Chapter 4

Washington Wrestles with Slavery

Perhaps no one better represents the complexities of slavery in antebellum America than Francis Scott Key who, for all the other things he did in life, might be some combination of amused and annoyed that he is best remembered for a patchwork poem set to an old Irish drinking song containing some of the most awkward bars in musical history. The Washington attorney and amateur poet was a reluctant slave owner, who freed his own slaves and represented for free African Americans attempting to buy their own freedom. Which in no way explains why he was such a sworn enemy of abolitionists, and a critical player in violent race riots in the city in 1835, in which a white mob roamed the city looking for black-owned property to destroy.

There is no way to know, or even logically deduce, how Key might have felt about the former San Francisco 49ers quarterback Colin Kaepernick, who sat during the pregame National Anthem in protest of police shootings in black neighborhoods. While Key was certainly on the side of freedom, loosely defined, and the rights of man, he was viciously opposed to agitation and anything that smacked of infringement on private property rights.

Washington's African American history is similarly complex, at times heartbreaking, at times inspiring, but always fascinating. Perhaps the best early example is Yarrow Mamout, an educated, likely upper-class African man of the Muslim faith from Guinea, who was enslaved at age sixteen and brought to Maryland in 1752, where he developed an expertise in a broad array of industrial arts. His owners—the prominent Beall family—allowed him to make money on the side, and at age sixty he was given his freedom outright, and told to go to work for himself. For Yarrow, sixty was the new forty. He was the owner of property, including bank stock and his own house in Georgetown, as he refocused his considerable talents from a world of gristmills and iron foundries to a world of finance. Yarrow would have been a familiar figure in Georgetown, walking the streets in his colorful kufis (his Muslim faith appeared to be considered as an interesting oddity, not a reason for persecution), and he was wealthy enough that he became a lender and was described in his later years as living quite a comfortable existence. He died, quite well respected, in 1823 and was buried in his home, in the corner of his garden where he would go every day to pray. His obituary noted that "it is known to all that knew him, that he was industrious, honest, and moral—in the early part of his life he met with several losses by loaning money, which he never got, but he persevered in industry and economy, and accumulated some Bank stock and a house and lot, on which he lived comfortably in his old age—Yarrow was never known to eat of swine, nor drink ardent spirits."

Yarrow's amazing story might have been lost save for two things. One, he sat for two artists in his old age, something that for a black man in early America was exceedingly rare. Charles Willson Peale, known for painting the great heroes of the Revolution, painted Yarrow at a time in the artist's career when he was fascinated by the aging process. Yarrow apparently sold Peale on the notion that he was in the area of 140 years old. In the portrait, Yarrow has a wise, bemused look and an enigmatic smile, not dissimilar to an aging Kobe Bryant. Today it hangs in the Philadelphia Museum of Art.

The second portrait, painted by James Alexander Simpson in 1822, shows Yarrow older and maybe a little worse for wear, hung in the Peabody Room of the Georgetown branch of the DC Public Library. In 2016 it was moved to the National Portrait Gallery on a three-year loan where it caught the eye of Washington attorney and writer James H. Johnston, who went on to write *From Slave Ship to Harvard: Yarrow Mamout and the History of an African American Family.* Johnston wrote that as late as 1948, the Peale portrait was misidentified as George Washington's personal slave Billy Lee, "the only African American a limited imagination could conceive Peale would have seen fit to paint."

According to period interviews, Yarrow twice saved up a comfortable nest egg, only to see it lost by the merchants he had invested it with for safekeeping. This was obviously getting disheartening, and Yarrow was concerned that he was growing too old to replenish his nineteenth-century 401(k) for a third time. But he did by baking bricks and weaving baskets and nets, and this time he was advised to purchase bank stock that set him up financially for the remainder of his life.

Of course, for African Americans, this success story was the exception, although how much of an exception is open to speculation. Yarrow's story is only remembered today because of the artwork, as black history in the nation's early years was not anything that white writers felt worthy of recording. Plenty of other success stories have certainly been lost. Indeed, a number of African Americans in Washington were considered noteworthy only when they were involved in a disturbance. The obvious example is Nat Turner, whose 1831 Virginia rebellion killed up to sixty-five whites (which whites more than retaliated for) and set the whole nation on edge wondering which enclave of slaves would rise up next to slit the throats of whites as they slept.

But since slaves were not generally given credit for thinking on their own, Washington's considerable class of free and educated blacks found itself under a cloud of suspicion as potential rabble-rousers.

Four years after Turner's execution, Beverly Snow was living in Washington, where he was widely acknowledged as having the most luxurious, delectable restaurant in the city. The Epicurean Eating House was located at the corner of 6th Street and Pennsylvania Avenue, and was emblematic of a thriving, free-black economy that would, again, prove not to be sticky in the American historical memory. Snow was also smarter, richer, better educated, and more talented than most of his white neighbors, which for an African American was always a dangerous mix.

Another dangerous mix was whiskey and talk of man's inalienable rights, a seditious cocktail that had overtaken eighteen-year-old Arthur Bowen, a light-skinned slave owned by Anna Thornton, a Washington socialite and wife of William Thornton, designer of the US Capitol. Any slave on a cotton plantation in the Deep South would have cheerfully traded places with the young man, or at least advised him to keep his mouth shut and appreciate his comparatively good situation. But Bowen would have argued, and not without reason, that while his present position might have been tolerable, it could change at any moment and he was powerless to control into what circumstances he was bought or sold.

It was not only whiskey that fueled his passions, although the liquor certainly helped. Bowen was a disciple of the Reverend John F. Cook, whose school at 14th and H streets included a smart, lively debate club prone to discussing constitutional rights. On a Tuesday night in early August 1835, Bowen staggered home, fuming over the unjust hand life had dealt him and trying to figure out what he was going to do about it. Somewhere along the way he happened upon an ax.

Bowen later claimed he had no memory of entering the bedroom where sixty-year-old Anna and Bowen's mother, Anna's personal slave, were asleep. Anna saw him first, swaying unsteadily in the room with the ax tucked into the crook of his arm. Aghast, she jumped from the bad, darted past him in the dim light and fled for help. The slave made no attempt to stop her. Arthur's mother, however, took matters into her own hands, snatching the ax and locking him out of the house, complete with a chewing-out for the ages. Anna arrived back home shortly thereafter with two prominent Washingtonians, and the group listened dumbstruck as the young man bellowed on about his rights, before disappearing into the night.

Even if sober, Arthur Bowen never could have imagined what he had just started.

The North had its abolitionists and the South had its plantations, but it was the nation's capital that had a strong dose of both—highly opinionated men representing the interests of their people. This tension permeated the upper classes; among the lower classes of whites something else was in play.

Throughout the South and in Washington, unpaid (slave) labor had a very predictable effect on the labor force: Paid work that was performed by low- or unskilled white workers in the North, scarcely existed in the South. Throughout Dixie, there were few jobs for poor whites, which led to an economic class that was not too much of a step up from the hand-to-mouth agrarians or hunter-gatherers of old. This was all the more evident in the cities, where unemployed whites saw blacks busy at work all day. For this misfortune, they did not blame slave owners or the institution of slavery—they blamed the slaves themselves and free blacks who, through industry, had managed to improve their lot in life.

In Washington, there existed a class of unemployed white men known as the Mechanics, who whiled away the days drinking heavily and looking for objects upon which to take out their anger. Bowen provided a convenient target. The Mechanics surrounded the jail where "Mrs. Thornton's mulatto" was being kept and threatened to tear down the jail and lynch its most infamous occupant. Anna meanwhile was distraught, not of her own plight but the plight of young Arthur, whom she tried hard to free without success.

Into this unsettled situation stepped the author of America's national anthem. Key was Washington's district attorney, who needed to figure out how to keep the peace in a city with a grand total of ten cops. To calm the situation, Key called the Navy Yard marines to Judiciary Square where, as Jefferson Morley wrote for the *Washington Post* in 2005, "the clamoring Mechanics were temporarily cowed but not calmed."

Key's views of slavery seem confused by today's standards, but in 1835 there would have been nothing particularly unusual about them, and given the nation as a whole they might have even been considered mainstream. Abolitionists opposed slavery, but that was often as far as it went. They no more wanted blacks living among them than today's animal-rights activists want to live in a rain forest. So to someone like Key who lived in the de facto Southern city of Washington, abolitionist troublemakers from up North were being patently abhorrent by telling Washingtonians that, not only would they lose their property, but that this property would be free to commingle with them on equal footing. Many opponents of slavery, Key and Abraham Lincoln to name two, felt that it would be best for all concerned if African Americans were repatriated in Africa.

Which is why Key wasn't content to let it rest with Arthur Bowen, but sought out the men who distributed literature that inspired slaves to think for themselves. As the budding crisis simmered in the hot summer days of August, he obtained a warrant for the arrest of a white physician named Reuben

Crandall suspected of possessing "wicked and malicious libel." Key sent a couple of officers to search the doctor's house; news of the mission was leaked to the public, and agitated Mechanics followed along. Crandall cooperated with the constables, who found copies of abolitionist newsletters that included the then-novel notion that slavery might drive the nation apart, to wit: "Then we are not to meddle with the subject of slavery in any manner; neither by appeals to the patriotism, by exhortation to humanity, by application of truth to the conscience. No; even to propose, in Congress, that the seat of our republican Government may be purified from this crying abomination, under penalty of a dissolution of the Union." The pamphlets also contain a rather cheeky response to those of Key's ilk, noting that native-born African Americans "have as good a right to deport [whites] to Europe, under the pretext that there we shall be prosperous and happy, as we have to deport them to Africa on a similar plea."

Crandall was carted off followed by the braying Mechanics to the jail, where again the marines had to keep the peace. If Key believed that the arrest of Crandall would satisfy the mob's bloodlust, he was disappointed. In fact, the two prisoners only served to double the crowd's anger. For the people and press, it was all coming together. The city had been flooded with literature from the Anti-Slavery Society, which had mailed 175,000 tracts throughout the country in July. (Postmasters in those days had the right not to deliver anything they did not like, and many exercised this right, understanding their incendiary nature.) Rather than causing those with proslavery sentiment to see the light, the pamphlets had the opposite effect. The loud barrage of the abolitionists was greeted with an even louder barrage of slavery sympathizers, and as evidence the city had the hapless Bowen and Crandall. Here was the obvious cause and effect: People like Crandall were handing out inflammatory literature and people like Bowen were reading it and going after old white women with an ax. In truth, while it was impossible to know Bowen's exact intentions, it seems clear that had he been intent on doing damage, there was little that a couple of aging women could have done to stop him. Yet according to the papers, he had all but hacked the respected Mrs. Thornton into tiny little bits.

For Crandall's part, he was socially active in the temperance movement, and while he opposed slavery he had little to do with abolitionists—his main side interest focused on botany. Rather than distributing abolitionist literature, he more likely had only received it in the mail. It is likely he agreed with the pamphlets and thought others would benefit from reading them, but he was hardly a wholesale distributer.

But the newspapers of the day didn't see it that way, and were more than happy to aid and abet mob sentiment. Nor did papers shy away from producing drama on their own. The *Washington Mirror* was only published sporadically during the years 1834 through 1836, but that was enough to inflict considerable damage on the city. As tensions mounted, the paper attributed to the restaurateur Beverly Snow comments insulting the wives and daughters of the Mechanics, specifically that he, Snow, could have any one of them he wanted. (Snow had the reputation as something of an egotist, so the comments attributed to him were entirely plausible.) Either way, the Mechanics were not of a mind to stop and ask for clarification. Three hundred to four hundred men surged to the

Epicurean Eating House, where their mood was not improved by learning that Snow had outfoxed them and slipped away to freedom, right under their very noses. Fueled by the contents of the bar, the mob took out its frustration on the establishment's fine furnishings and appointments. The mob was about to burn the restaurant to the ground when someone pointed out that the building itself was owned by a white person, and that it would be disrespectful to destroy the property of a man against whom they had no gripe.

This information temporarily stalled the Mechanics' momentum, but soon enough the mob turned its attention to the school of Reverend Cook. The Mechanics' anger blossomed into a full riot as they destroyed the school, several churches that were home to free blacks, and a couple of nearby apartment buildings before they set fire to a brothel. The more levelheaded people of Washington were appalled, and, there being a shortage of police and military forces, a counter-mob began to gather to keep the Mechanics from getting even further out of hand. (Snow had had it with these white savages; he packed up and fled for the safety of Canada.) The rest of the city pinned their hopes on President Andrew Jackson, who was just returning to town from a Southern sojourn. Old Hickory's presence calmed the Mechanics, but there were still two men in jail awaiting trial to be dealt with, not to mention the leaders of the Mechanics, whom Key was prosecuting, notwithstanding that he himself had been somewhat responsible for firing them up.

A jury took no time whatsoever to sentence Arthur Bowen to hang. Key, the opponent of slavery, had argued for the death sentence, while Anna Thornton, the slave owner, did everything in her power to save him. She called in every chit available to a woman of Washington's high society—editors, publishers, senators, congressmen, and Vice President Martin Van Buren. Her impassioned, seventeen-page letter to President Jackson asking for a pardon still exists. Arthur was languishing in jail writing mournful poetry about his impending demise when the marshal rattled the lock on his cell and told him that the president of the United States had finally succumbed to Anna Thornton's pestering; he would go free, from jail if not from enslavement.

Unlike Bowen, who blamed himself, Crandall was convinced that he was the victim of fake news. While the literature had indeed been found in the doctor's house there was no evidence that, as Francis Scott Key claimed, Crandall was the ringleader that led to the August violence. Nevertheless, the case went to trial. *U.S. v. Reuben Crandall* was the most sensational trial in Washington in years," wrote Jefferson Morley in the *Washington Post*. "The newspaper coverage was extensive. The courtroom in City Hall was crowded. Several congressmen took front-row seats."

In Crandall's view, Key was a weird duck. The prosecutor, he wrote, trusted no one and no one trusted him, due largely to his schizophrenic approach to slavery. However, Key's motives were best understood not in terms of Crandall, but in terms of personal and professional practicalities. Within the abolitionist movement, there were those who argued for freedom and assimilation into American life, and those who argued for freeing and colonizing the former slaves in Liberia. As is often the case, this interfaction feud was particularly bitter, and the Abolition Society's literature, which chided those in favor of colonization, was in Key's view particularly offensive. Perhaps more importantly, on the political side, it was as dangerous for a politician in the 1830s to be seen as soft on slavery as it was to be seen as soft on crime in the 1990s. Key's prosecution of Crandall was designed as much as anything to affirm President Jackson's anti-abolitionist street cred.

Key's strategy was to put the abolitionist tracts on trial and hope that Crandall could be convicted of guilt by association. But while he could prove the "offensive" content of the literature, he had no direct evidence that the young doctor was in any way connected with their publication. Worse for Key, his own duplicity in the issue of slavery came back to bite him. To everyone's confusion, defense lawyers read a scathing rebuke of slavery into the record, which was counterintuitive to say the least, since it was antislavery sentiment that was on trial. The judge finally interrupted to ask what was up with *that*, and Crandall's attorney announced that the incendiary words had, years earlier, been written by Francis Scott Key himself in a treatise on colonization. The judge winced, and confessed that he assumed these words had come from the very tracts that Key was accusing Crandall of distributing.

It was an absolute dagger to the heart of Francis Scott Key's case, and the author of the *Star-Spangled Banner* knew it. Stammering, he attacked the relevancy of this evidence, to which Crandall's attorney innocently admitted he merely wished to state the abolitionists' position, and Key's was the most artful language on the subject he could find.

In the end, Key simply had no evidence linking Crandall to the tracts, beyond simple possession. After a ten-day trial, the doctor was quickly acquitted. Unfortunately, during his extended stay in the filthy District jail awaiting trial, he contracted the tuberculosis that would kill him two years later. Nor did the verdict itself settle anything. Washington continued to feel very strongly both ways about African Americans in the workforce and with regard to their race in general, passing codes that limited the types of jobs that free blacks could hold, even as Congress was (if only for show) mildly limiting the practice of selling slaves within the city. And, of course, Washington remained a ground ripe for political exploitation on the issue. Northern abolitionists were aware of the symbolism of the nation's capital, and funded operations large and small to disrupt slavery's ecosystem in the city.

So inundated was Congress by zealots on both sides of the issue, that in 1836, lawmakers voted to wash their hands of the entire matter—as if they could. In a self-imposed gag order, Congress resolved that that "all petitions, memorials and papers touching the abolition of slavery or the buying, selling, or transferring of slaves in any state, district or territory of the United States be laid upon the table without being debated, printed, read or refined and that no further action whatsoever shall be had thereon." It was perhaps the only time in American history that Congress decided voluntarily to shut up. But it hardly mattered, as abolitionists bypassed Congress and began illegally freeing slaves on their own.

The largest organized escape plan was carried out in April of 1848, and the same time, ironically, that Washington was (somewhat prematurely) celebrating the new freedoms that they supposed were being bestowed upon the people in revolutionary Europe. As the great political orators, many of themselves slave owners, spoke in the glow of celebratory bonfires of freedom and the rights of man, more than seventy-five slaves were putting these thoughts into action. Late on a Saturday night, from both sides of the Potomac, they silently made their way to the sixty-four-foot cargo schooner *Pearl* courtesy of two white men, Daniel Drayton, who chartered the ship for one hundred dollars, and Edward Sayres, the captain of the boat. Another key player in organizing the escape was John Bent, a man born in slavery who had purchased his freedom and went on to found and serve as the first pastor of the John Wesley AME Zion Church. (His son Calvin was a groundbreaker as well, becoming the first African American architect in the city.) Many of these slaves who boarded the *Pearl* would not have fit the standard field hand stereotype, as these men and women were not assigned to hard labor. Washington slaves were more likely to be butlers, drivers, housekeepers, and valets. Some were educated and had ties to families of American icons with names such as Madison, Webster, and Polk.

But for a little breeze, the *Pearl* might have made it the 230 miles from Washington down the Potomac to the Chesapeake Bay and up and then north to New Jersey and freedom. In the early morning hours, however, the ship stalled in the calm darkness, and it was all the crew could do to keep the incoming tide from sucking it right back up to the dock from which it had departed. When the sun rose, there was the *Pearl*, right in front of some of the busiest wharves of Alexandria. A wind finally stirred, but by then it was too late even on a quiet Sunday morning. A taxi driver, who was miffed at being stiffed by a runaway with no coins for payment, sold out the operation. The *Pearl* was tracked down near Point Lookout at the mouth of the Potomac, where it had anchored to ride out a storm.

The escape attempt again raised the bile of proslavery factions, who rioted for three days against the abolitionist *New Era* newspaper, and stormed the jail trying to haul Drayton and Sayres out of jail for a summery hanging. But the city beefed up security just in time, and the street thugs had to be content with criminal convictions of the two men (pardoned four years later by Millard Fillmore), who were prosecuted by none other that Philip Barton Key II, Francis Scott Key's son, and a man reputed to be the handsomest in all of Washington at the time. But if his father had been consumed by the issue of slavery, Philip was consumed by the issue of womanizing.

As improbable as the whole *Pearl* affair had been, its final and perhaps most bizarre twist didn't occur until a decade later, when the younger Key became involved with a woman named Teresa Sickles, the wife of one of America's greatest scoundrels, a corrupt congressman named Dan Sickles. Key and Teresa had a rendezvous point in a black neighborhood on 15th Street, and for a length of time Dan never noticed, probably because he was carrying on so many affairs of his own. Then one day an anonymous letter arrived in the mail, outing the happy couple, and enraging Sickles, whose temperament was seldom on firm footing to begin with. Armed with two pistols, Sickles murdered Key in broad daylight near what is now Lafayette Park. An O. J. Simpson–scale trial ensued—Dan forced Teresa to hand-write a full confession, which was dutifully reprinted in *Harper's Weekly*—and Sickles was acquitted by employing the nation's first-ever defense of temporary insanity. Forced to choose between the equally repugnant Sickles and Key, the public and press seemed genuinely stumped. But the consensus was that whoever got the ball rolling by sending the poison-pen letter exposing the 15th Street tryst site was a genuine hero. No one to this day can say who sent it, but historian Mary Kay Ricks, author of *Escape on the Pearl*, turned up a compelling tidbit: A house in the black neighborhood on 15th Street was among the assets listed in the will of none other than Zion church pastor and *Pearl* conspirator John Bent.

Washington continued to be the epicenter for both proslave and antislave voices, in the years leading up to the Civil War, as well as a convenient lightening rod for those wishing to make a political statement. Two years after the *Pearl*, New York abolitionist William Chaplin raided the capital, making off with two slaves owned by Representative Robert Toombs of Georgia, who would go on to be the Confederacy's first secretary of state. The hijinks came to a quick end, as the carriage of runaways was quickly hunted down. Chaplin was jailed, but he was bailed out by Gerrit Smith, the great abolitionist from New York, who also bankrolled a forlorn little community of freed slaves in the Adirondack Mountains, as well as John Brown's 1859 raid on Harpers Ferry. Back in New York, Chaplin had no intention of returning south for trial and Smith, if he cared, which he probably didn't, lost his bail money.

Even the *New York Times* blasted Chaplin's little trick, a viewpoint for which the paper itself took considerable heat. The editors were finally compelled to explain: "We believe slavery to be an evil, quite as earnestly as any of our censors. We wish some feasible plan could be devised to get rid of it. We believe that it is deeply injurious to any society in which it exists, and that it deprives subjects of rights which belong to them in common with the whole human race. We hope the time will come when all parties and classes of men in this country will . . . devise some means whereby the rights of the slave can be restored."

All this ink devoted to lofty ideals was rendered inert by the *Times'* steadfast belief that none of it mattered because slaveholders' property rights came first. No matter how well intentioned Chaplin may have been, his commando raid was "an outrage and a wrong." Striking a blow at what was legally defined as property, the *Times* believed, would only hardened the Southern resolve and make "Southern masters jealous and suspicious of the North, and give color to the belief that the North was willing to aid a crusade against their institutions and rights."

While the editors "wouldn't lay a straw in the way of the advancement and improvement of the colored race," they wondered how ex-slaves would fare on their own, "helpless and friendless" and dependent on Northern charities for their existence. The *Times* wanted an orderly plan by which slaves would be freed, their masters compensated and ex-slaves educated and assimilated into society in an orderly society. And everyone just needed to sit tight and hold their tongues while this was allowed to play out. As John Brown would prove eight years later, that was way too much to ask.

In Washington, oddly enough, it had almost gone as the *Times* had foreseen. By the middle of the nineteenth century, there were twice as many free blacks as slaves in the city, and the abolitionist movement was gaining steam. By 1844, Congress had repealed the gag rule. In 1849, an obscure congressman from the frontier introduced legislation that would have treated enslaved Washingtonians almost exactly as the

New York Times had prescribed. But at that point in his career, no one was paying any attention to Abraham Lincoln, and the bill went nowhere. The Compromise of 1850 contained language that prevented the introduction of slaves into the city for resale. Two years later, Harriet Beecher Stowe published *Uncle Tom's Cabin*, and even though many Southern jurisdictions censored the novel, there was scarcely a slave owner alive who didn't possess a copy, hiding it under his bed as if it were porn, and reading it voraciously when no one was watching to see if there was any character he recognized. The *National Era* newspaper that had been targeted by mobs following the *Pearl* incident serialized the book following its publication, making it easily available to everyone in Washington.

More antislavery legislation was introduced in the following decade, but none was successful until a bill in the spring of 1862—one year into the Civil War, and after Southern lawmakers had vacated the city—freed 3,100 enslaved men, women and children living in the District. Slave owners could claim up to $300 in compensation, and—as proof that the US government still had a way to go on race relations—the freed slaves themselves were offered $100 if they would be so good as to leave the country. On the sunnier side, ex-slaves who had purchased the freedom of a loved one were themselves eligible for compensation. Fair is fair. A follow-up bill designed to tie up some loose ends regarding compensation permitted slaves to be called to testify in court if there were a conflict over ownership. This set a precedent of allowing African Americans to participate in the judicial process on equal footing with whites, something that had scarcely been the case beforehand.

All told, it cost Congress one million dollars to buy out the Peculiar Institution within the District. With the war continuing to rage, former slaves in Washington remained wary. It wasn't until the fourth anniversary of the legislation, in 1866, that a true celebration commenced. Half of the African American population turned out for a joyous parade and speeches. The event was captured by poet James Madison Bell who wrote:

Unfurl your banners to the breeze!
Let Freedom's tocsin sound amain,
Until the islands of the seas
Re-echo with the glad refrain!
Columbia's free! Columbia's free!

James Greenleaf was the Federal City's Founding Speculator. The dubious financial instruments he created to buy and sell investments would sound quite familiar to modern-day wolves of Wall Street. *Courtesy Library of Congress.*

The commercial mind of George Washington wanted the Federal City to be a comprehensive city with a lively port and impressive public works. He supported this elegant design by Pierre Charles L'Enfant. *Courtesy Library of Congress.*

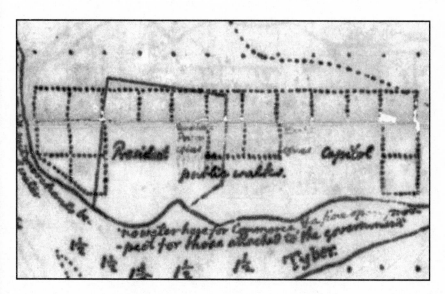

Thomas Jefferson didn't want a government capital that was in any way ostentatious, and he did not want it located in a place that was easily accessible. His sketch of a proposed capital is significantly more spartan than L'Enfant's. *Courtesy National Endowment for the Humanities.*

Financier Robert Morris as painted by Charles Wilson Peale. Morris was known as the financier of the American Revolution, but by the end of his career he was spending his days in a Philadelphia debtors' prison. The legislature felt so bad about this circumstance that they changed bankruptcy laws to allow for his release. *Courtesy Library of Congress.*

Vice Admiral Alexander Cochrane offered slaves freedom in exchange for fighting in the British army during the Chesapeake campaign. This Corps of Colonial Marines saw action in the Battle of Bladensburg, which would have terrified white Americans who were always in fear of armed slave uprisings. British Rear Admiral George Cockburn said the troops performed "unexpectedly well." *Courtesy National Portrait Gallery, London.*

Cartoon entitled "The Fall of Washington—or Maddy in full flight," lampooning the mad dash of President James Madison out of the city and into the Maryland countryside as the British army approached. *Courtesy Library of Congress.*

CAPTURE AND BURNING OF WASHINGTON BY THE BRITISH, IN 1814.

British troops were bewildered that they did not meet more resistance when they marched on Washington in the summer of 1814. Before setting fire to the White House, they ate a sumptuous dinner intended for the President Madison and his cabinet. *Courtesy Library of Congress.*

A PEEP AT THE FUTURE.

Cartoon portraying a "Whig Fantasy" shows John Tyler out of office as an organ grinder begging for pennies, as Whigs occupy the White House. Tyler's Secretary of State John C. Calhoun would have been particularly galled at the woman's garb and speaking with in a negro dialect. *Courtesy Library of Congress.*

A Nathaniel Currier lithograph of the USS *Princeton*. The ship was rigged to sail, but its main form of propulsion was screw propellers. The steamer's funnel telescoped to avoid detection. *Courtesy Wikicommons.*

The slave of a prominent Maryland family, Yarrow Mamout was painted by Charles Willson Peale at a time when people of color in America were seldom singled out for special treatment. *Courtesy Philadelphia Museum of Art.*

The backyard of the house in an African American neighborhood where Teresa Sickles and the son of Francis Scott Key carried on an affair. Mr. Sickles was not pleased. *Courtesy Frank Leslie's Illustrated Newspaper.*

Even though they were freed in 1862, former slaves in Washington did not dare celebrate their freedom until after the end of the Civil War. *Courtesy Library of Congress.*

The office and staff of Washington's Provost Marshal during the Civil War. The office had an uneasy truce with the city's brothels, and ranked Mary Ann Hall's as among the best, with eighteen "inmates." *Courtesy Library of Congress.*

The Treasury Building at the time of the Civil War. Inside would have been towering stacks of money, towering racks of guns, and something even more unusual—women. *Courtesy Library of Congress.*

Francis Spinner remembered that his wife and daughter were good with scissors. That led him to the unprecedented step of staffing the Treasury Department with women. *Courtesy Library of Congress.*

Through no particular skill of his own, Lafayette Baker lucked into a job as head of Washington's national police. He tried to dig up dirt on the Treasury Department, without much success. *Courtesy Library of Congress.*

President Grant, shown here as an acrobat delicately balancing his many liabilities, including Orville Babcock in the lower right. *Courtesy Library of Congress.*

Railroad speculator Jay Gould was the leader of what became known as the Gold Ring, but he divested just before the hammer fell. *Courtesy Library of Congress.*

Jeanette Rankin of Montana was America's first female congresswoman. She also made history for voting against two world wars. *Courtesy Library of Congress.*

Construction of the National Cathedral lasted the better part of a century. Designers wanted to convey an image of strength but were leery of excess decoration. *Courtesy Library of Congress.*

Frederick Law Olmsted Jr. was the son of the great landscape architect who designed Central Park. To some, the son was the more accomplished designer of great gardens. *Courtesy California Department of Parks and Recreation.*

Glastonbury Thorn on Wearyall Hill in England, before its limbs were stripped by vandals in 2010. *Courtesy Ken Grainger for Wikicommons.*

CHAPTER 5

The Best Little Business
in Washington

"Fighting Joe" Hooker was a passable Union general in the Civil War, best remembered for two things, both misnomers. One was the nickname "Fighting Joe." While Hooker might indeed have been more aggressive than the chronically passive Federal commanders who came before him, the nickname was the product of a typo in a newspaper headline. The dispatch was intended to read "Fighting—Joe Hooker Attacks Rebels" but somehow the dash was omitted prior to publication.

The more obvious legend is that General Joe Hooker's partiality to late-night parties that were well attended by ladies of the evening gave rise to the lowercase noun for women of that profession. It's certainly plausible enough, but the term "hooker" was first used in 1845 at a New York harbor protected by a hook-shaped spit of land. However, it's quite likely that this little local colloquialism would have been lost to history had not Fighting Joe come along and reinforced it so emphatically.

The conflict that tore the nation asunder was detrimental for many concerns and institutions, but it had the opposite effect on the world's oldest profession. "The Civil War was the primary cause of the largest increase in the sex trade in the nineteenth century, perhaps the single greatest spurt of growth in the nation's history," wrote Catherine Clinton in her book *Public Women and the Confederacy.*

Hookers were not so much known as "hookers" then as they were known as "public women," and the profession was regarded as legitimate enough to have its own category in the US Census. This label, however, had more than one meaning. Besides the obvious, public women were public women because, well why not, they didn't hold themselves to the conventions that governed their more genteel sisters. They would walk the boulevards without an escort, show up at taverns and the theater, wear lipstick and rouge, and behave in all manner of ways that would give society women a case of the vapors.

Prostitution of course had always been simmering beneath the surface, but it exploded during the war. By 1864 there were more than five hundred brothels in the greater Washington, DC, area, employing as many as 7,500 women. To put this in perspective, the total population of the District in 1860 was just 75,000. Prostitution during the war was rampant, even in erstwhile honorable and chivalrous Southern cities such as Richmond.

Some of this was driven by supply and some by demand. The war drew recruits for duty from far and wide, including toughs from the cities and innocents from the countryside, all of whom were potential customers. For the soldiers from the city, prostitution would have seemed routine, but one can only imagine the reaction of legions of kids who had never even shaved and had seldom set foot off the farm, and whose mammas had almost assuredly never warned them that such an enterprise existed. If some of these wide-eyed chillins' were tempted, others were clearly horrified. Clinton quoted one Southern soldier who wrote, "The state of the morals is quite as low as the soil, almost all the women are given to whoredom & the ugliest, sallowfaced, shaggy headed, bare footed dirty wretches you ever saw." As a personal aside, Clinton noted that "this is perhaps the harshest statement I have ever read by a Confederate soldier about southern white women—so conditions must have been appalling to make him drop all pretense of chivalry."

But while young men with a little bit of pay in their pock-ets, no wife or family on hand and, between battles, weeks and even months of epic boredom, might naturally seek out sexual favors, there was also an economic incentive for women to offer their services for sale. Numbers are understandably scarce, but it's believed a substantial number of women in the South resorted to prostitution because they had little other choice. The rural South was largely a cashless society, meaning that whatever a family ate was the sum product of whatever it was able to grow or shoot. With most every adult male called to war, even this sketchy existence was jeopardized. Prostitution could mean survival. "For many Civil War-era women, prosti-tution was an inevitability, especially in the South, where basic necessities became unaffordable on the salaries or pensions of enlisted husbands and fathers," Angela Serratore wrote in *Smithsonian* magazine.

In the North, too, female heads of destitute families might turn to prostitution for lack of other opportunity. But others went into the profession guns blazing, so to speak, because prostitution could mean not just survival, not just a comfortable life, but an outright fortune and an element of status. In New York, a woman could earn between five and ten dollars a week at prostitution, compared to two dollars a week for a domestic or factory worker. Those women with "legitimate" work might still find themselves short of the funds it took to feed, clothe, and house a family, if they were the sole breadwinner.

The sex trade was also the best, if not virtually the only, way for women in the mid-1800s to build wealth. If a woman owned property in New York City in that time period, there was about a 40 percent chance that the property was a brothel. Nowhere was prostitution as an element of female upward mobility more apparent than in the Wild West.

"When women were barred from most jobs and wives had no legal right to own property, madams in the West owned large tracts of land and prized real estate" wrote Thaddeus Russell in his book *Renegade History of the United States*. "Prostitutes made, by far, the highest wages of all American women. Several madams were so wealthy that they funded irrigation and road-building projects that laid the foundation for the New West."

This would be apparent in the District as well which, along with soldiers, had a ready-made customer base in the nation's political class. This leads to another point, being that not all brothels were created equally. In Washington, there was the vice district known by the picturesque name of Murder Bay, with all the charms that vice districts are typically known for. This contrasted with more upper-crust brothels, whose creature comforts and cuisine would put the average city hotel to shame.

Civil War officers had different ways of dealing with prostitutes—when they weren't patronizing the industry themselves. Indeed, they as a rule had no real problem with prostitution, because anything that would keep the men happy was generally regarded with acceptance if not outright encouragement. And practically speaking, prostitution was difficult to eradicate. Waves of merchants known as sutlers followed armies around like flies on a donkey, selling food, booze, clothing, trinkets, paper, pencils, dice, cards, and anything else a soldier might desire. Along in this traveling city were hookers who would come streaming back almost from the instant they were chased away.

The generals would have been more tolerant if not for the venereal diseases that were part and parcel of the trade. In the Civil War, more men died of disease than from battle wounds, and while not necessarily deadly, syphilis and gonorrhea sidelined otherwise capable soldiers. (Not to mention that mercury, the "cure" for the disease, often left men worse off than they had been previously.) Plus, a man who had become incapacitated getting his jollies occupied just as much hospital bed space and care as a man who had heroically had his leg blown off in battle, a circumstance which struck hardly anyone as fair.

This roundabout intolerance reflects the extent of sexually transmitted disease during the war—generals might have been able to overlook a handful of cases, but literally thousands of men were being put out of commission. Historians estimate that between 8 percent and 10 percent of the men became infected, which might be a reasonable reflection of the number of all the men who visited prostitutes.

Officers had different ways of handling the scourge. The most storied, and entertaining, occurred in Nashville, Tennessee, where the war had seen a sevenfold increase in the number of city prostitutes since the war's inception. In 1863, Union Major General William Rosecrans was occupying Nashville when he decided the hookers had to go. And by go, he meant *go*, as in more than two hundred miles up the Cumberland and Ohio rivers to Louisville, Kentucky.

The most hapless individual in this whole episode was not a hooker, it was a man by the name of John Newcomb, who had just slapped the last coat of varnish on his spanking-new steamship, the *Idahoe*. He might have had great commerce planned for his ship, but its first assignment, per military order, was to ship more than a hundred prostitutes upriver to Louisville. Newcomb complained that such a mission would ruin the reputation of his boat, and in this he was quite correct as the *Idahoe* forevermore became known as the S.S. *Floating Whorehourse*. Worse, when he got to Louisville, the city fathers made it clear that Newcomb's cargo was to stay right where it was, forcing him to steam north to Cincinnati where he received much the same reception. Lacking provisions and any other plan, Newcomb turned the *Idahoe* astern and began floating back down the river—his passengers plying their trade to anyone brave enough to swim.

Back in Nashville there had been much rejoicing as the *Idahoe* disappeared around the bend, the papers crowing that this abomination had been scrubbed from the city streets once and for all—the miscalculation being that almost as soon as the white prostitutes vanished, black prostitutes arrived to take their place. After reflection, the papers and the city council decided that the original condition might not have been so bad after all, and when the white women disembarked from the returning *Idahoe*, the Army and the city came up with a Plan B to deal with the problem of prostitution: They legalized it.

And it worked. Public women received physical exams, and if they passed they were issued, for a small fee, a certificate of health. If they were diseased, they were treated for free in one of two city hospitals designated for that purpose—one for men (known as Hospital 11), one for women (known as the Pest House). Everyone was happy. The city was happy, the officers were happy, the men were happy, and the prostitutes were happy. The only person not happy was the hapless Newcomb, who tried without avail to win recompense for a ship full of soiled mattresses and other nasty souvenirs from the *Idahoe*'s unsuccessful journey.

In Washington, the job of putting a lit on prostitution problem fell to—what could go wrong?—Fighting Joe Hooker. When the war had broken out, Hooker, a retired Army officer, had been in California trying his hand at farming. Largely due to military politics, Hooker was not immediately welcomed back into the Army. But with the defection of so many officers to the South, leadership was in demand, and Hooker was awarded a division in 1861 and assigned to guard the Federal City.

This was important work, as the threat to Washington was very real. In the summer of that year, the Union had been routed at the Battle of Bull Run, just a few miles south of the city. And President Lincoln could stand outside the White House and see the flag of the Confederacy flying across the Potomac River in Alexandria, Virginia.

By this time, Murder Bay had already made a name for itself. Today it's known as Federal Triangle, a wedge of land between Pennsylvania Avenue and the National Mall, home to some of the city's greatest museums and art galleries. But on the eve of the war, it was a greasy collection of bars, flophouses, gambling halls, brothels, and assorted shanties that could proudly go toe to toe with any slum of its kind in the nation. Accentuating the squalor was a fish-gutting concern, a number of privately owned hog pens, and a broad canal that had become little more than an open sewer that transported offal, human waste, and the occasional animal carcass to the Potomac. The slum's additional fairly sizable tracts of open land, meant it had the potential to get much worse.

That happened with the arrival of the war when thousands of soldiers garrisoned in the city or were passing through on their way South wanted one last fling before engaging in the somber work of battle. Soldiers and suppliers packed the city (seeking shelter, new Union recruits would curl up in the hallways of the newly built Capitol) and added significantly to the demand for vice.

Hooker's concerns were similar to those of Rosecrans, although more than disease he was concerned about the availability of his officers and men. With brothels scattered about the city, it was taking the general too much time and effort to round up his subordinates from beds located in so many quadrants of town. He solved this by herding as many of the brothels as he could into Murder Bay, where one or two messengers could efficiently round up his wayward troops when the alarm sounded. The vacant land quickly filled to capacity with even more brothels, gambling houses, and the thieves, muggers and desperadoes that come with the territory. At times, it could seem as if Washington's red-light district were only slightly less dangerous than the bloody fields of Gettysburg and Antietam, and the area duly took the name of "Hooker's Division," a moniker that lasted into the 1900s.

The police too were often outflanked. "From Missouri Avenue on the east to [Hooker's] Division on the west, police duty in the Mall triangle was no plush assignment," wrote Donald E. Press, in the *Record of the Columbia Historical Society.* "Time after time officers had to haul surly gambling house operators or kicking prostitutes off to a nearby paddy wagon. Sometimes the policemen did not come away from such experiences unscathed. Called to quell a row at Mollie Mason's bawdy house on Thirteenth Street in October 1863, Officer Viehmeyer performed his duty only after being struck squarely in the face with a chair."

There was no real playbook for handling soldier-female relations. Treatment of women in the Civil War was, to say the least, uneven. In New Orleans, Major General Benjamin Butler issued Order #28, which expressly gave soldiers permission to punch women who were behaving badly right in the snout. Offended residents of the city responded by painting Butler's likeness in the bottom of their chamber pots. Authorities in Washington, for their part, tried some of the same tactics as Nashville. Followed by a brass band playing "The Rogues March," police drove a large band of crooks and prostitutes onto a waiting train for a trip out of town. This, of course, scarcely put a dent in the problem.

The city also considered the idea of legalization and licensure. But unlike in Nashville or New Orleans, where such measures had proved to be successful, the City of Washington depended on Congress for authorization, something a majority of the council viewed as a nonstarter. In a debate at City Hall, one council member, according to the *Evening Star*, noted that "the proposition would shock the country members [of Congress], as it was so adverse to decency and propriety . . . the members from the interior would certainly not vote to license [prostitutes]." However, another councilman, according to the *Star*, responded that "members of Congress were the best customers of such places. He did not think they would be much shocked." the council kicked around the problem for a while longer without result, but was amused by the fact that any time the topic of prostitution came up "the reporters would take extensive notes."

Washington's bawdy houses took on a wartime flair, with names like the Ironclad, Fort Sumter, and Headquarters USA. Whimsy and crudeness went hand-in-hand in the Division, often with results as comical as they were ghastly. Historian Thomas P. Lowry wrote about a family named Light, whose father, mother, and three daughters engaged in a rather unsavory family business, the daughters being peddled by their parents to the public at large. "On one occasion, they were all arrested when the Lights had hired an organ grinder [and his monkey] to provide music for a Dance of the Seven Veils, performed by the three Light girls and attended by a large crowd of appreciative soldiers," Lowry wrote. "The soldiers' shout of encouragement created such a racket that the police were called, and the entire Light family, the organ grinder and the monkey were all brought before the magistrate."

During the war, wrote Linda Wheeler in the *Washington Post*, "the District was a wide-open city where upwards of 10 percent of the residents made their living as prostitutes. Their houses were in the heart of official Washington: one block from the White House, down the street from the Capitol and across the avenue from the National Theatre."

And the criminal justice system had little impact, despite all its best efforts. The city police force was outnumbered by prostitutes on the order of thirty-three to one, not to mention that it paid a lot better to be a public woman than it did to be a man in public service. Penalties were notoriously light, despite the efforts of some judges to lay down the law. In June, 1864, the *Evening Sun* reported on a judge's soliloquy on the state of affairs in the nation's capital. Things had gone downhill "on account of the worthless character in the army around here," and that "the jury owed it to themselves, their wives and daughters and sons to use all their power to put down this crying evil of prostitution. Public women, devoid of all character, stalked abroad through our public places, thus driving honest and good women away; and every effort should be made to put down this vice. The nymphs of prostitution, with pointed effrontery occupied the public haunts of business, and insulted honest women."

Prosecutors picturesquely sermonized against "faded and filthy wretches" and the customer who "returns like a dog to his vomit." While willing to excuse the country soldier who got swept up by forces beyond his control, that gave no quarter to the one "who finds his native element in these dirty waters and [spends] a lifetime in degrading and debasing human nature."

Yet not all of Washington prostitution rings reeked of rotgut and sweaty sheets. Late in the twentieth century, the Smithsonian began work on the National Museum of the American Indian at a location south of the National Mall, four blocks from the Capitol. Prior to construction, archeologists led by Dr. Donna J. Seifert sifted the ground for evidence of meaningful history, and they were rewarded with a curious find: a dump filled with shards of expensive dishes, residuals of fancy foods, and hundreds of corks from high-end champagne. These were the vestiges of one of the best bordellos in the District, a luxurious hall of plush furniture, fine art, delectable cuisine, soft beds and feather pillows and certainly none of the riffraff that frequented Murder Bay. There would be no crowds of drunken soldiers braying for the Light sisters to "take it off!"

This was the property of Mary Ann Hall, a madam of elite status, compassion and taste, and, last but not least, a keen mind for business. By the time of her death in 1886, her estate approached an inflation-adjusted $2 million. The papers were good enough not to state precisely how she became so wealthy and so beloved; they only mentioned that she had. "With integrity unquestioned, a heart ever open to appeals of distress, a charity that was boundless, she is gone but her memory will be kept green by many who knew her sterling worth," said the *Evening Star*.

The *New Republic* newspaper referred to her somewhat cryptically as "an old-time Washington figure." Hall, the paper noted, "was well known at one time, and kept an establishment of national renown. . . . In addition to the real estate in this district, she was the owner of a fine farm in Virginia, and besides household furniture and chattels, she left $57,200 in government and railroad bonds. She had been living quietly at her farm for many years, but returned lately to her old mansion in this city, living there in entire seclusion and respectability."

Newspaper readers at the time would have known how to read between the lines, and would have understood that respectability had not helped her accumulate all those railroad bonds. While her more lowbrow contemporaries complained, her upscale clientele of congressmen and military officers protected her from judicial proceedings, although she was in fact no stranger to the inside of a courthouse. As early as 1844, she showed up on the police blotter. On February 20, 1864, the National Republican briefly, very briefly noted that Hall had been indicted of running a bawdy house, and convicted by a jury the next day. It is also possible Hall's brand extended beyond Washington. A brief item in the July 22, 1866 *New York Times* reports that "Mary Ann Hall was convicted of keeping a house of bad repute at No. 19 Laurens-street [the city's red-light district]. White girls lived there and colored men patronized the establishment. She was sentenced to one month in the Penitentiary and fined $50."

But if some papers were willing to gloss over her indiscretions, others, such as the *Evening Star* found the juicy details too good to pass up. An officer for the prosecution on one of her court cases testified that hacks came and went at Mary Hall's establishment with brow-raising regularity. The customers of these taxis were almost exclusively male. "He had seldom seen females alight," the *Star* reported. What he had seen tumbling out of the house was a contingent of the Anderson Zouaves, a volunteer infantry regiment from New York, which had been passing through the District early in the war on their way to a trying campaign designed (unsuccessfully) to capture the Southern capital of Richmond. Witnesses reported that the house was sumptuously appointed, with fine furniture, rich carpets, and an enviable collection of art, all of it "first class [and] very showy." The front entryway was equipped with a heavy iron ball and chain that prevented the door from opening more than a few inches while allowing the Chinese servant to assess whether the visitor was friend or foe.

During Mary Hall's trial, detectives recalled visiting the house over the years, usually to investigate reports of stolen property, a missing person, or difficult customers who neglected to pay the hacks. Hall must have felt relatively secure in her relationship with the law, as one detective recalled her calling for the law from an upstairs window to "take away a colonel." This appeared to suggest a potentially awkward situation, as detectives had to determine how high-up an officer it was safe to haul off to the guard house. In fact, it was not unknown for officers and madams to go into business together.

It also has to be said that, for reasons that are open to speculation, the detectives did not show the same prosecutorial zeal as did the city's judges, who viewed prostitution as such a scourge. Yes, the cops on the beat shrugged, there were an inordinate number of women hanging out at the place, no, they hadn't seen any "implements of industry" to suggest these girls were duly employed, yes, when detectives happened by at ten in the morning it looked as if the women "had just got up" and yes, hacks were coming and going late into the night with regularity. But, you know, there's really nothing to see here; it could be anything.

While judges could rail against prostitution from on high, it seems apparent that those who knew Mary Ann Hall personally were fond of her. She was also notoriously discreet. Her clientele could count on her to keep their secrets, and considering how high-profile was the customer base she served, it's rather remarkable that there were few public scandals perpetuated by her establishment. Hall also seems to have been well served by a good heart—in later life she turned her bordello into a women's clinic. In the historic Congressional Cemetery are buried many of America's luminaries—senators and congressmen, lawyers, generals, poets, explorers, Indian chiefs and musicians. But among the most impressive monuments is one that bears the name of Mary Ann Hall, buried there with her mother and sisters. And more certainly among some of her best customers.

Chapter 6

Treasury Girls—The Original Rosie Riveters

The North didn't win the Civil War because it had better soldiers, it won because it had better bureaucrats. By definition, the Confederate model reason-for-being was small, decentralized government which, whatever its merits might be, isn't terribly efficient if you're trying to win a war. Many Southern soldiers went hungry not because there was no food, but because tons of it rotted on train-station platforms for want of a coordinated government transportation network.

But where the South really lost the war was in the area of finance. It had no centralized tax collection and no unified currency. Under Secretary of the Treasury Salmon P. Chase, however, the Union put in place a modern monetary system that largely remains intact to this day. Both sides printed up copious amounts of cash, but the Union raised taxes, sold bonds, and backed its currency with gold, so its paper money inspired confidence. In the Confederacy, by contrast, the currency was little more than Monopoly money, with nothing of value behind it. The proof was in the inflation rate, which through the course of the war was 9,000 percent in the South, but only 80 percent in the North.

It is possible to get a sense of the enormity of the war effort through the sheer physical amount of paper money it took to pay for it, and the manual labor needed to produce all that paper.

At the beginning of the war, Chase browbeat Northeastern banks into lending the Union $150 million in gold, to be secured with government paper paying 7.3 percent interest. But producing a government security was not a simple task. Prior to the war, the government contracted the job to New York printing houses, which took up to two months to complete the order. According to an essay by historian Franklin Noll, "The securities were printed from one to four [certificates] per sheet, and upon reaching the Treasury, the sheets were bound in a book. Then, whenever a security was sold, a clerk in the Register's office would perform the proper record keeping and, taking a pair of scissors, cut the security out of the book. The security would then pass to the Register for his signature. Next, it went to the Treasurer's office. There, more record keeping would occur, and the Treasurer would sign the security. The duly signed security would then pass to the Secretary's office, which might record further information and pass it along to the sealing room. A clerk would emboss the Treasury seal on the security, marking its authenticity. The security was then ready for issue."

This was tedious enough when the government's standard annual issue was $10 million. Since $50 million represented 4.3 million pieces of currency, the job of signing and applying a seal to each one was staggering. One by one, Treasury got rid of the formalities; recording was scaled back, the embossed seal was eliminated and clerks were deemed good enough to sign the bill (a printed signature would come later). Even so, the job was taking seventy clerks signing three thousand pieces of currency a day to stay current. And the government's money machine was just getting warmed up. When no amount of threats was adequate to squeeze another dime from the banks, President Lincoln and Congress fell back on an idea from Illinois businessman Dick Taylor to print paper currency that, like Treasury notes, would be legal tender, but unlike Treasury notes, would pay no interest—in other words, cold, hard cash.

These greenbacks helped win the war, but they initially had all the logistical problems associated with the bonds. Already crushed with work—and with little hope of reinforcements because the war was taking every available man—the clerks were suddenly asked to cut, trim, and sign $150 million in greenbacks, which amounted to twenty-five million bills. Someone needed to come up with an idea as innovative as the greenback itself to keep the government functioning.

But where was the desperately needed manpower to come from?

Although Chase gets the credit for innovation at the Treasury Department during the war years, it was really Treasurer Francis E. Spinner who did much of the grunt work.

With men frantically being recruited to war and, quite literally, tons of paperwork to be processed by a depleted staff,

Spinner came up with an idea so radical that it finally had to be approved of by President Lincoln himself—the Treasury Department would hire women.

Twenty years prior, during a stint at the Mohawk Bank, Spinner had noticed something: Women were better with a pair of scissors in their hands than men, so he had put his wife and three daughters to work cutting and trimming bank notes with satisfactory results. He understood that society felt he had "peculiar ideas" regarding women in the workplace, but that didn't prevent him from taking his plan to Chase. Spinner later wrote that he told the secretary that "these young men should have muskets instead of shears placed in their hands, and be sent to the front, and their places be filled by women, who would do more and better work."

Chase didn't like the idea, but he took it to Lincoln. Lincoln was skeptical, but the facts were the facts. Men were needed to fight, and as a practical matter, if Treasury were to fund the war effort, it needed more hands on deck. One other matter recommended itself to women in the workplace. Alexander Hamilton, in a report to manufacturers seventy years prior, had urged the acceptance of women in industry not necessarily out of enlightenment, but because they would work more cheaply. Hamilton was right. The first women hired by Spinner did the same work as the men, but at six hundred dollars a year, or about half of what an entry-level man was paid.

The first to be hired in the spring of 1862 was Jennie Douglas of Ilion, New York, upon whose slight shoulders rested nothing less than the future of women in the American workplace. The bills had to be neatly trimmed to be acceptable for general circulation, but the work was more demanding

ing the bill. The story was that the superinten-
tructed to put "Clark" on the note, with everyone
to be understood that this was to be William, of
Clark fame. But since no one specified, Spencer
ed people were talking about him. (This story is
ainly false. There are two other more plausible
s, but both are so colorless that they scarcely bear

was assisted in his office by a staff of five, four of
re girls in their teens or early twenties, and this was
er sensed an area ripe for exploitation. He had his
ak into the boarding house where the girls roomed
through their diaries. He arrested the girls separately
ing each that the others had confessed, threatened
would rot in prison if they didn't do the same. All
onfessions that were not necessarily based on reality,
ining in the public's eyes all the same. It was here that
rvened, to the detriment of one of the girls, but to the
ge of the others—and of Clark (Spencer, not William).
tral to the story was the unfortunate Maggie Duvall
he papers agreed, made for an attractive corpse, even
final hours had been traumatic. Duvall was a typical
ry employee—young, ambitious, and from a family
cted well enough to know someone who could recom-
her for work. But during the course of her employment,
eveloped a cough that kept getting worse. Finally, in the
g of 1864, she died at age twenty-one of what her doc-
said was a pulmonary illness. The bereaved family was
wing the horse-drawn hearse to the cemetery when seem-
out of nowhere, Baker stepped in and ordered it to turn

than it sounded. The heavy shears were sixteen inches long, and constant use caused blisters to pop, leading the women to quip that they too had bled for their country. Douglas was not just adequate, she excelled, and was soon cutting and trimming faster than any of her ham-handed male colleagues. "Her first day's work settled the matter in her and in woman's favor," Spinner said. Her performance gave Spinner cover to hire another handful of women.

Not since the Four Horsemen of the Apocalypse, perhaps, had such a small workforce been subjected to such scrutiny. So unusual was the circumstance of federal female employment that newspapers reported the names of women as they joined the staff—On October 9, reported the Longmont (Colorado) *Daily Times*, Miss Fannie L. Halstead, Miss Annie York, Miss Belle S. Tracy, Miss Elizabeth Stoner and Miss Mary Burke came on board. Before the year was out, Douglas had been joined by seventy other women at Treasury.

Men in general seemed nonplussed by the development, their angst quelled only by the assumption that this was just a wartime phenomenon, and that when peace returned, so would the women return to their kitchens and laundry rooms.

But as time went by, the Government Girls were almost something of a tourist attraction. Soldiers stationed in the capital remarked on the sight of throngs of young women reporting for work, with no small degree of amazement. While black and lower-class women might be seen working the fields or mills, "respectable" upper- and middle-class white women were almost never seen in the common workplace. For the Treasury Girls, the impetus transcended patriotism. The jobs paid far better than any factory and domestic situation, although the high cost of living in Washington during the war took an over-sized bite out of the women's paychecks.

Most women came from families with some degree of status, and had names that would be widely recognized in the city. But as in any broad demographic, there were bound to be, as one Union officer put it, some "black sheep." And as the war was winding down and the Rebel cause less of a threat, the capital's fearmongers turned their attention to the disturbing situation of women who were permitted, paid no less, to work side by side with men.

Colonel Lafayette C. Baker was a failed prospector during the California Gold Rush and Union spy who took a job in the Lincoln Administration as, essentially, the chief of Washington's secret police. Appointed by War Secretary Edwin Stanton, Baker had broad and largely independent powers to investigate evil wherever evil's path might take him. "Lafayette Baker's exploitation of Union paranoia in the Civil War set an unfortunate precedent," wrote US intelligence officer Michael J. Sulick. "In the last two years of the conflict, Baker rounded up hundreds of suspects, trampled civil liberties and missed genuine spies operating not only in the Union government, but also in his own counterespionage service." Some years later, Sulick wrote, a congressional investigation related to the impeachment hearings of President Andrew Johnson determined that "it is doubtful if Baker has in any one thing told the truth, even by accident."

In his role as chief of Washington's secret police it was almost inevitable that Baker would become focused on the Treasury Department and alleged corruption—misappropriation always a possibility in any establishment dealing in mountains of cash.

In the event of a Rebel [...] the most important building [...] Capitol or White House. Th[...] out politicians; it couldn't wi[...] Treasury workers were organi[...] a visitor would have noticed o[...] and one big room stacked with [...] in that particular era, would hav[...] surreal.

For Baker, it was all too much [...] ruption (the cynics of the day sug[...] the case because no one at Treasur[...] offer him a cut) soon bled into an [...] pitude. Women couldn't be trusted [...] men could be trusted with money.

Before Congress got wise to Bake[...] partner in crime, and the bungling s[...] of Representatives to join him in a sl[...] the foul temptresses who must certainl[...] halls. By 1864, Representative James [...] would later be censured for bribery) was [...] and millions of the public money" had [...] project, and that the Treasury Departme[...] into "a house for orgies and bacchanals."

Baker's target was probably not so much [...] but the superintendent of the National [...] Spencer M. Clark. It is also quite probable t[...] was not that he was crooked, but that he wa[...] tendent would also find himself in hot wat[...] for printing up mass quantities of five-cent n[...]

image ador[...]
dent was in[...]
assuming it [...]
Lewis and [...]
Clark figu[...]
almost cer[...]
explanatio[...]
repeating.
Clark [...]
whom w[...]
where Ba[...]
goons br[...]
and rifle[...]
and, tel[...]
that the [...]
signed [...]
but da[...]
fate int[...]
advant[...]
Ce[...]
who, [...]
if her [...]
Treas[...]
conn[...]
men [...]
she [...]
spri[...]
tor[...]
fol[...]
in[...]

around. The investigator said he had discovered that while at her Treasury job, Duvall had become involved with a coworker who happened to be the son of a prominent judge.

Baker produced witnesses who testified that Duvall "was in a family way" and was being cajoled into an abortion by the would-be father. The young man was accused of murder, along with another young woman who secured "medicine" that was to assist with the abortion. When the medicine didn't work at first, Duvall was given a heavier dose that proved to be fatal, Baker alleged. A jury was convened, but after a full day of testimony, there was no verdict. At four in the afternoon, the jury told the judge that the only way to settle the matter was an autopsy. The judge agreed, much to the consternation of the family, which—having already witnessed the interruption of the young woman's burial—protested wildly against any further desecration of their loved one.

Conveniently, the corpse was being kept right in the next room for safekeeping, while the criminal justice process worked through the thorny questions at hand, and immediately on the judge's order, Maggie's sister ran to the room and threw herself on the coffin, her hysteria reaching a point where she had to be physically removed. Even the salacious *Evening Star*, which was not easily moved, had to admit that "the scene for a few moments was very painful."

A team of doctors descended on the body, and in a couple of hours they had their answer: Maggie Duvall died of pneumonia brought about by chronic consumption. She was not, and had never been pregnant, and according to a majority of the doctors present, "the character of the deceased as to chastity [was] fully vindicated." Baker, accused of "a barbarity rarely surpassed," was taken down a peg, but the spy and his host of serial perjurers did no small amount of damage to the reputation of the Government Girls by swearing that girls agreed to share their favors as a condition of employment.

Maggie Duvall was at last laid to rest in a rosewood coffin with silver handles and lined with white satin, a wreath of white flowers on her head, and a beautiful camellia in her hand as it lay across her breast.

As the funeral showed, Government Girls obviously were not factory girls, but the daughters of families of means. This, however, did not protect them from gossip, and in truth might have contributed to the reasons that so many people seemed to be rooting for scandal. It goes without saying that the majority of men at the time felt threatened, irritated, outraged, or all three at the thought of women encroaching upon the professional places of business. They seemed to fear that purposeful marble halls would be overrun with lace, blossoms, and nosegays should the "fair sex" intrude on these nineteenth-century man caves. "Ballgowns and coquetries" in the office, wrote one critic, had no place in the business world, because not only would women fail to carry their weight, they would be a distraction to the earnest males who were only trying to do their jobs.

Nor were men the only critics of the new development. In Richmond—where spare manpower was far more scarce than it was in the North—the government printers adopted the Yankee model of hiring female trimmers, much to the chagrin of Southern diarist Mary Chesnut, who pledged, "Survive or perish—we will not go into one of the departments. We will not stand up all day and cut notes apart, ordered round by a department clerk. We will live at home with our families and starve in a body. Any homework we will do. Any menial service— under the shadow of our own rooftree. Department—never!"

Even in the North, where the first national suffrage organizations were only a few years away from organizing, not all women were on board. Journalist Jane Swisshelm, who seemed as if she should be a proponent of the practice, had quite a catty view of the Treasury Girls. They were either Southern sympathizers; old biddies trying to make themselves look younger by filling in their wrinkles with pipe clay and batting their eyebrows in a most horrifying way; or the love-starved daughters of aristocrats who were less interested in getting to work on time than they were cooing at their male counterparts and, Swisshelm maintained, generally acting "like a duck in a thunderstorm"—whatever that was supposed to mean.

Swisshelm was more charitable in her analogies toward the many young government women who were "pure as a New England frost, bright as a button, active as a bee," and did as much or more as any man in the department. The problem here, she said, was that the best workers tended to have no influential families behind them, so they could be fired over the pickiest mistake. Also, wrote historian Mary Elizabeth Massey, "rumors were repeatedly circulated that the women employees in one or another of the departments were to be fired, but there was no wholesale dismissal during the war. Congress discussed the matter during the winter of 1865–66. It was the opinion of many that they should be replaced with retiring soldiers, but public sentiment was divided."

As the number of women at Treasury grew (nearly 450 women were employed by the war's end) and proved their mettle, the Government Girls did have one somewhat perverse circumstance working in their favor: They were still paid roughly half the salary as were the men, or between $600 and $720 a year. This fact alone made them somewhat indispensable, not to mention that male workers were hard to find at any wage. The women of course were well aware of this discrepancy, as they were of the leverage in their possession. During the war, women in the Bureau of Printing went out on strike demanding better pay and won an extra sixteen dollars a month. When the war was over and the men returned home, this bargaining power was lost, and women would not receive another pay raise through the course of the next two decades.

But eighty years before Rosie the Riveter was to celebrate women in the workplace, the Treasury jobs had opened up a possibility for women that had not existed before, and spawned some interesting stories as well. In 1860, young Grace Bedell of Westfield, New York, became famous for her letter to Abraham Lincoln that began, "I am a little girl only 11 years old, but want you should be President of the United States very much so I hope you won't think me very bold to write to such a great man as you are." As a girl, she would not be permitted to vote even had she been old enough, but she promised that she would, should Lincoln decide to let his whiskers grow, try to talk her four brothers into voting for him in the upcoming election. The rest is history, of course, but this would not be the last time young Grace corresponded with Lincoln. In 1864, when she was fifteen, Grace wrote to tell the president that her family had fallen on hard times. Perhaps the man who grew a beard on her recommendation would now give her a job: "I have heard that a large number of girls are employed constantly and with good wages at Washington cutting Treasury notes and other things pertaining to that Department. Could I not obtain a situation there? I know I could if you would exert your unbounded influences a word from you would secure me a good paying situation which would at least enable me to support myself if not to help my parents, this, at present—is my highest ambition."

It does not appear that the young woman came to Washington to work, but Lincoln, after his initial skepticism, would routinely recommend women for positions, signing slips of paper for the women to present to the supervisors when they asked for a job.

And it almost goes without saying that a number of women who went to work for the government were remarkable in their own right. At age eighty-one, Emma Graves of Bloomville, New York, was still working for Treasury in 1918, fifty years after she got her start in the redemption center where worn notes were turned in to be destroyed (in those days old bills were chopped into pulp and fashioned into souvenirs). Graves bitterly complained when she was transferred to Register's office one year before she was to celebrate the golden anniversary in the office where she had gotten her first and only job.

Unlike soldiers who served during the war, the women who did their share for the war effort received no pension, so lengthy careers were often necessary. Nor were the jobs particularly secure once the war ended. In 1882, Treasury employee Rebecca Wright got wind that her job was about to be taken away from her and given to a male applicant. Her boss apparently did not recognize that he was not just dealing with Rebecca Wright, he was dealing with Rebecca Wright, Heroine of Winchester.

General Phil Sheridan was a controversial, ill-tempered knot of a man who attended West Point, where he failed in math and was accused of an overall poor attitude. He was suspended for fighting—maybe not the worst thing for a potential soldier—and finally graduated in the bottom third of his class. Lincoln, who, where his generals were concerned could be incredibly forgiving if they were good, playfully called Sheridan "a brown, chunky little chap, with a long body, short legs, not enough neck to hang him, and such long arms that if his ankles itch he can scratch them without stooping."

But in the summer of 1864, Sheridan had a problem. He was driving this cavalry south toward the city of Winchester, Virginia, where the North had few friends and there was consequently little intelligence concerning the forces under Confederate General Jubal Early. But he'd heard of a woman, a schoolteacher, who was also a slavery-hating Quaker and might be counted upon to provide the whereabouts of the rebels. That woman was Rebecca Wright, who on a summer afternoon answered a knock on the door to discover the slave Thomas Laws, who had a permit to cross Confederate lines to sell vegetables. Wright invited him in and Laws spit out a piece of tinfoil that he was to swallow if discovered. Wrapped in tin was a slip of tissue with a request for intelligence. Somewhat nervously Wright complied, and the general used the information from the schoolteacher to drive the rebels out of the Shenandoah Valley.

After the war, Sheridan sent Wright a gold watch and promised he would never ever forget her heroism. Now, with her Treasury job on the line, it was time for Wright to see if Sheridan were a man of his word. She picked up a pen and wrote Sheridan, explaining her predicament. Sure enough, the general roared to her defense explaining in no uncertain terms to Treasury Secretary James Folger that without Wright's intelligence the North might not have gained the upper hand in time to ensure the reelection of Lincoln and all of history might have changed. Wright kept her job, retiring in 1914 after forty-seven years of service.

Women were asked to perform all manner of tasks, particularly in the redemption center where unclaimed funds were disposed of and damaged money replaced. For example, an Ohio farmer named Ypsilianti Smith, who was not in the habit of trusting banks, spent his adulthood burying his savings in the ground. At some point he realized the vessel in which he was storing the gold and silver certificates was not offering adequate protection from water and worms, and made arrangements to get the stash to Washington for exchange into recognizable currency.

The logical thing to do, would have been to box up the crock and send it to Treasury, but here the old farmer's distrust came back to bite him yet again. He somehow got the idea that the most inconspicuous way of transporting the bills was to dump the decaying, brittle notes into a pillow case, which he strapped to his torso before donning multiple layers of clothing and tacking up his horses in order to personally accompany his savings to Washington. His strategy was a success in the sense that he was not robbed along the way. Unfortunately, his method further pulverized the bills, not to mention that they became doused in sweat, a substance not known for its properties of preservation. Even with all that, the women at Treasury sorted it out and issued fresh bills to restock the farmer's savings, which in today's money amounted to a somewhat astonishing $400,000. To show his appreciation to the dedication and hard work of the Treasury women, Ypsilianti Smith sent them a bag of grapes that the girls actually seemed pretty happy to get.

A somewhat sadder version of a similar story occurred with the death of a tramp, who was subsequently buried in a pauper's grave. A death notice that was published to alert any surviving relatives came to the attention of the dead man's brother in Germany, who felt there might be something more to the story. So strongly did he feel this way, that he came to call upon an undoubtedly skeptical coroner, whom he convinced to exhume the body. What the brother knew was that this "tramp" was actually a wealthy man, and sure enough, an examination discovered the modern equivalent of $133,000 stitched into his clothing.

The woman at the center of these stories was Mrs. Willard Leonard, the widow of a Civil War soldier who had come to Treasury during the war—delayed somewhat because the Confederates had burned the bridge she needed to get from her home in Pennsylvania. She was a squat woman with a pile of black hair on her head, a fair complexion and, noted the *Washington Times*, "sharp piercing black eyes that might disconcert a person bent on tampering with government money."

But it was not in the redemption department that Mrs. Leonard made a name for herself. Her unique talent came in the form of a photographic memory that proved to be particularly useful to the government for ferreting out counterfeit bills. She explained her uncanny powers this way: "I glance at an article and with that one glance am able to to say whether it is perfect. I can also remember for an indefinite period what the imperfections were."

As much as a hair on the head of a Founder that was out of place set Mrs. Leonard's antennae to quivering. One had to be sure of her work, because if a counterfeit bill slipped through, the inspector would have to pay an equivalent amount of cash out of her own pocket. Many tried to take Mrs. Leonard down, and they all failed. On occasion, it would appear to the cash room, the Redemption division and even the Secret Service that the widow had erroneously flagged a good bill. But deeper investigations always proved her right, and she became known as the Sherlock Holmes of Treasury.

On the insistence of her physician, Mrs. Leonard retired in 1911, at the age of seventy-one. "I have given the government the best years of my life, and I do not regret it," she told the papers on her retirement. Many women—those initial Treasury Girls, and those who gained employment in other government offices that followed Treasury's lead—felt the same. And the man they admired most was Francis E. Spinner, the Civil War treasurer who gave the girls a chance. On Spinner's death, the Government Girls raised $10,000 and bought him a monument that was placed in Myers Park in Herkimer, New York. "We never forgot Treasurer Spinner," Emma Graves told the *New York Times* in 1913. "We felt we owed the appointment of women to him." On the stone is Spinner's conviction that "the fact that I was instrumental in introducing women to employment in the offices of government gives me more real satisfaction than all the other deeds of my life."

CHAPTER 7

The Most Corrupt Man in a City Full of Corruption

When Vice President Dick Cheney's chief of staff I. Lewis "Scooter" Libby was indicted in 2005, it marked the first time in more than a century that a sitting senior White House aide had faced such an indignity. It might be something of a wonder that it hasn't happened more often in a city that has been home to more than a few president-whisperers, people who view themselves as untouchable—and more apt to take risks—because they have the full faith and credit of the man in charge. Some get into trouble for acting as presidential hatchet men, as did Bob Haldeman and John Ehrlichman who were convicted of obstructing justice following their resignations during the Watergate era. (Men such as these are notoriously difficult to purge from there national consciousness. Haldeman wrote a bizarre tell-all book that one reviewer said "proves virtually nothing but the crumminess of everyone concerned" in the Watergate era, while Ehrlichman appeared in an ad for Dreyer's Grand Ice Cream, which was immediately pulled after the public reacted with horror.)

Other aides stumble because they have their own infatuation with power and take advantage of a weak president. Even when there is no criminal mischief afoot, Washington has always been intrigued, and at times infuriated, with its Rasputins, the ones behind the scenes pulling the president's strings. Certainly, Cheney himself would seem to fit into this category, as does Donald Trump's chief strategist Steve Bannon.

But in the eyes of history, these are amateurs. For the king of the White House puppet masters it is necessary to go back to the 1870s and the administration of Ulysses S. Grant, a reluctant president who sought office only to prevent his military victory over the South from being unraveled by conniving politicians. He'd witnessed too much bloodshed to permit that to happen.

Through the course of the war and the course of his presidency, Grant was served by a loyal aide named Orville Babcock. Babcock was born in the farthest northern reaches of Vermont in 1835, still at a time when—with New York and Philadelphia to the South and Montreal and Quebec to the north—this particular neck of the woods would have been considered to be the heart of the continent. He was born into a military family of some acclaim, his grandfather having served in the Revolution and his father having helped repulse the British in the War of 1812 in the Battle of Plattsburgh.

With such a legacy, he was accepted into West Point, where he graduated third in his class in 1861, shortly after the opening shots of the Civil War had been fired. Orville Babcock had a brilliant, if morally rudderless, mind that seemed to have little care whether it was working on the side of good or evil. He entered the Army Corps of Engineers just about the time it was dawning on Washingtonians that they had a war on their hands, and very little in the way of defenses to keep the Visigoths—or Virginians, take your pick—from storming the palace gates.

Geographically, the city offered some defensive problems. It bulged like a canker below the Mason-Dixon Line, with its immediate neighbors on three sides of dubious loyalty. Residents could see Rebel flags fluttering across the Potomac. So dicey was the situation in Maryland that Lincoln had secessionist lawmakers arrested and imprisoned, with nothing in the way of constitutional niceties being afforded to the hapless prisoners. With the advance of weapons technology, it would be child's play to level half of Washington from the banks of the Potomac in Northern Virginia. Big cannons were now capable of heaving projectiles five miles or better, and such was their accuracy that gunners liked to brag that they used bushel baskets for target practice. To top it off, the Blue Ridge Mountains were like an arrow aimed at the heart of the District. Confederate armies could (and did) use these long, high ridges to screen their movement from the Yankees as they demonstrated against the Union capital.

Still, Washingtonians had a hard time believing they were in any real danger—until a July day in 1861 when residents packed their picnic hampers and trundled thirty miles south to a rural railroad crossing where, they assumed, they'd be treated to the sight of the dashing Union Army putting its boot on the throat of the Rebels. Instead, the Confederates chased the Yankees all the way back to the city, the terrified soldiers' retreat slowed only by traffic jams of civilian carriages desperately searching for safety.

As it became apparent that this would not be an afternoon skirmish but an all-out war, stern, white-haired Army veterans such as General Joseph Mansfield, said in no uncertain terms that the city needed to defend itself for an inevitable Rebel onslaught. Mansfield would die a year later at the Battle of Antietam, so he was no position for I-told-you-so's when the Confederates eventually came calling in 1864, but defend itself Washington did. Among the engineers called on to do this important work was Orville Babcock, who had earned high marks for building and guarding a pontoon bridge at Harpers Ferry that gave the Union army a route to a Rebel stronghold at Winchester, Virginia.

The young engineer was among the thousands of soldiers who were garrisoned within Washington's boundaries where, lacking proper barracks, they slept (and cooked and ate and drank and belched and scratched themselves, but seldom bathed) in the US government's finest office buildings, including the Capitol. Heloise herself wouldn't have had enough hints to remove all the stains and filth these soldiers left behind when they finally vacated. Remedies such as vinegar and sand were needed to scrub the Capitol to the point where it was presentable when Congress reconvened.

The threat of invasion proved it is indeed possible to get Congress to act in a hurry. The legislature immediately appropriated funding to protect itself, and Babcock was among the engineers called on to ring the city with sixty-eight forts, ninety-three batteries, twenty miles of rifle pits, and thirty-two miles of military roads surrounding the capital. Entire forests were leveled to prevent the Confederates from launching a surprise attack. So generous was Congress in spending funds to protect its own hide that, according to the National Park Service, "Washington became the most heavily fortified city in the world."

The city was abuzz as it had never been before. If nothing else, the Civil War made Washington feel important, an emotion it was not entirely used to.

Historian Margaret Leech wrote, "an alien activity was imposed on the slow life of the city. Its rough pavements were noisy with the clatter of army wagons, the screams and curses of the drivers, and the crack of their long whips. Every house and every hotel was filled. Sutlers had taken all the vacant shops. Business revived. Even property holders felt encouraged. The depot and the wharves knew a ceaseless passing of horses, cattle, wagons, ambulances, provisions, arms, equipment, uniforms—all the multiple requisitions of a government at war."

In short, the Civil War had transformed Washington from a sleepy Southern town into an industrious Northern city. And in the end, it would not be time wasted.

The most celebrated element of this defensive network was what became known as Fort Stevens. It was built on Vinegar Hill just inside the city's northern boundary, which was home to a community of free blacks, including a woman by the name of Elizabeth Thomas. Thomas and her family members owned the highest ground in the area, which unfortunately for them, meant that this was where the fort would be built.

Standing beneath a sycamore tree and holding her six-month-old baby, she sobbed as soldiers tore down her home and barn, and ripped up her gardens and orchards. At some point, Elizabeth became aware of a lanky figure in black at her side, and watching the scene unfold offering her what comfort he could. "It is hard," Abraham Lincoln acknowledged. "But you shall reap a great reward." The president was right and wrong. Thomas went on to flourish after the war, but no thanks to the government, which only compensated her with a payment of $1,835 in 1916, a year before her death.

Lincoln would be back at Fort Stevens—against everyone's wishes, for fear for his safety—in 1864 as the South made one last, desperate gambit to turn the tide of a war it was badly losing. With the bulk of the Confederate Army pinned down at Petersburg, Virginia, General Robert E. Lee sent the crusty and canny General Jubal Early north through the Shenandoah Valley with orders to create chaos where he could. Early was the man for the job. Contending that he was demanding payment for Union atrocities in the Valley, he ransomed some Northern towns and burned the ones that didn't pay up.

The first week in July, Early saw the opportunity he was after—the chance to cut sharply to the east through Frederick, Maryland, and hook down to attack Washington, which was lightly defended, having sent its best troops south.

Early's entire campaign had been a surprise to the Yankees, and the notoriously underfed Southern army was now living high on the hog, raiding Northern kitchens of their delicacies and Northern wine cellars of their hooch. And they might have done real damage to the Northern capital had it not been for an unimpressive band of green soldiers under the command of General Lew Wallace, who would go on to write the novel *Ben Hur*. Wallace tripped up Early's advance at Monocacy

Junction just enough to prevent a coordinated Southern attack on Washington. The Confederate general looked longingly at the city's defenses, but in the end decided an attack just wasn't worth the risk.

By this time Babcock, having served well in the Eastern and Western theaters of the war, had settled in as General Ulysses Grant's aide-de-camp. Babcock had caught Grant's attention at the siege of Vicksburg, a decisive Federal victory in the West, and the Union general counted heavily on his right-hand man on the drive to capture Richmond. Babcock was also entrusted with running dispatches between Grant and General William T. Sherman as the wiry redhead marched relentlessly to the sea. It was Babcock who delivered Grant's demand of surrender to Lee, and escorted the great Southern commander back to Grant's headquarters.

Babcock was dark haired, with a red goatee and friendly blue eyes, which tended to belie any criminal intent. Grant historian Allan Nevins described Babcock as "quick, alert, impetuous, daring, with the mien of a dashing soldier and the manners of a gentleman . . . dexterous at turning a compliment or launching a sarcastic shaft, he was a formidable foeman. He was full of resource; defeated at one point, he would spring to another." In his obituary in the *New York Times* he was remembered as "a very genial, hospitable man [who] was generally well-liked wherever known." It was telling that when Grant, who did not have a reputation as a dazzling socialite, was invited to a party, he would frequently send Babcock as his grinning, glad-handing replacement.

Upon Grant's election to the presidency in 1868, he again called on his trusted friend to be what we would now call his chief of staff. It was a logical choice. Babcock was smart, loyal, well organized and effective. But at thirty-four, he was also young and ambitious, and he apparently saw his appointment as a way of cashing in on his military service.

The new president had been a tremendous judge of soldiers, a skill that didn't translate into the civilian world. He was, by all accounts, scrupulously honest, and it seemed never to have occurred to him that a person in whom he had placed his trust would turn out to be any different. He also might not always have been as engaged as he could have been. Of the presidency, Grant wrote Sherman that "I have been forced into it in spite of myself."

Postwar America was also a different place, and changing more rapidly than Grant, and many others, could keep pace with. Industry and expanding frontiers meant fortunes to be had, and Babcock wasn't the only young man looking to hit it big. It was an age of railroads, land grabs, high finance and speculation, and it was a storm perfect for corruption. Grant had total trust in Babcock, which allowed the Army engineer to position himself, quite literally, between the president and the public. From a desk just outside Grant's office, Babcock was the less-than-scrupulous conduit—just as he had been between Grant and Sherman—between the president and America's financiers from the dark side. "The various Grant scandals had little in common except for the hand of the ubiquitous Babcock," wrote Timothy Rives for the National Archives' *Prologue Magazine*. "'The eternal cabal—with Babcock always at the centre!' wrote one despairing historian of the administration."

And in the private sector, Babcock had plenty of company. Jay Gould might not have heard of hedge funds and high-frequency trading, but he would have been right at home in those environs. The railroad speculator was a deliciously corrupt individual, whose evil is best savored at a distance of a century and a half. Gould outswindled the likes of Vanderbilt, Fisk, and Drew; he was just as happy to double-cross his friends as his enemies; his shenanigans in the markets ruined many an innocent man; and, while he has his defenders, about the best thing that most historians have to say about him is that he had the good grace to die at the relatively young age of fifty-six.

About the only person to get the better of Jay Gould was the fabulous British fraud Lord Gordon-Gordon, who in 1870 duped the tycoon into thinking that he was a cousin of the wealthy Scottish Campbell family, and made off with a one-million-dollar bribe of Gould's (to steer Campbell investments his way). The rogue fled to Canada, with Gould himself, along with a posse that included three future congressmen and two future governors, hot on his trail. They kidnapped Gordon-Gordon, but were stopped by Canadian Mounties and tossed into the calaboose without bail. Upon hearing of this outrage, thousands of Minnesotans volunteered for a military invasion off Canada, until negotiations succeeded in the release of Gould & Co.

At this point, the loss was more about pride, because thanks to a swindle the preceding year, Gould would have been flush. The Civil War was financed in the North with paper money, but with hostilities at an end the Grant Administration was steering the nation back toward a gold standard, buying up the nation's greenbacks with hard currency. While the government had plenty of gold, there was a limited amount available on the open market, and Gould and his partner James

Fisk conspired to drive up the price, reckoning that it would encourage western farmers to produce more crops for export, a fact that would happily benefit Gould's Erie Railroad.

Gould and Fisk set out to buy up all the gold they could, but while they felt comfortable manipulating the private markets, they needed help stopping the Grant Administration from releasing new allotments of gold to the public each week. For this assistance, they went to Grant's brother-in-law Abel Corbin, Assistant Treasury Secretary Daniel Butterfield and of course the reliable, in some aspects, Orville Babcock. Together they helped convince a skeptical Grant that farmers would indeed be helped, and the president ordered an end to the weekly one-million-dollar gold sales on the public markets.

This in itself was a jolt to investors who were counting on sanity returning to the gold market. Gould and his friends, Babcock included, had been buying up every ounce they could get their dirty paws on, and as gold skyrocketed, many on Wall Street who did not believe the price could hold were shorting the metal, or effectively betting that the price would come down. But when Grant cut off the gold tap, the price spiked, ruining more than a few seasoned investors.

Gould and friends, meanwhile, were amassing a paper fortune just on the price of gold alone, not to mention any future profits from increased shipping on Gould's railroads. But at some point, the profiteers—Grant's family, business associates, and staff—might have been better off had they stopped harping about the benefits of limiting the circulation of gold. So insistent were they that the president began to smell a rat, and he said as much in a letter advising his brother-in-law to steer clear of Gould and Fisk.

Shortly afterward, Grant flooded the market with gold, and the bottom fell out of the market, ruining speculators who had been bullish on specie and sending the stock market plunging by 20 percent. Known as Black Friday, it ruined any number of established traders and sent the economy into a two-year funk. Some of the people hurt the most by the Gold Ring, ironically enough, were the farmers whose cause it had purported to champion.

To the astonishment of everyone, the list of casualties did not include Gould, who had learned of Grant's plan from Corbin and secretly sold off his positions in gold. He had neglected to mention this detail to his closest associates, including Fisk and Babcock. Fisk made out OK, successfully arguing in court that he had not approved of gold purchases ostensibly made on his behalf. Babcock, a small fish swimming with sharks, did not. He lost the equivalent of $800,000 and had to place his house into hock to stay afloat.

At roughly the same time, Babcock was also losing a battle on the international front. He'd been sent by Grant to investigate the possibility of annexing the Dominican Republic (known then as Santo Domingo) into the United States primarily for a place to send former slaves in the South who were struggling under Reconstruction. Babcock, like Grant, was a strong believer in Reconstruction and by extension some semblance of civil rights, and for this he deserves credit. Unfortunately, where Babcock was concerned, things were never that simple.

Unbeknownst to Secretary of State Hamilton Fish, Babcock, egged on by a couple of speculators who had formed the Santo Domingo Company in New York, drew up an annexation treaty with Dominican President Buenaventura Báez. It was much like modern circumstances where a president and rookie staff member have issued executive orders without consulting the agencies the orders were to affect. Congress and members of Grant's own cabinet alike were flabbergasted at the secret mission. The only unanimous, or almost unanimous, support came from the Dominican people, who voted in favor of annexation by a margin normally reserved for tin-pot dictators: 15,169 to 11.

Fish and Interior Secretary Jacob Cox pointed out that Babcock had no official standing in government, and likened it to some random tourist visiting the Caribbean and coming back stateside with plans to annex an island. In the first cabinet meeting after Babcock's return, Fish threatened to resign and Cox noted that there had not been so much as a discussion over whether annexation was a good idea or not. In the annals of embarrassing presidential moments, this would have at least been in line for an honorable mention. Grant waited for someone to speak up in his defense. No one did.

But the former general didn't win wars by backing down. In November 1869, he again sent Babcock to Santo Domingo, this time with official State Department status, but without the knowledge of Congress. Again, treaties were drawn, but this time it was the US Senate's turn to be indignant. Perhaps the larger problem was that Grant and Senator Charles Sumner— back at his desk after being literally beaten to within an inch of his life on the Senate floor by Representative Preston Brooks in 1856 after speaking hotly against slavery—were bitter rivals battling for control of the Republican Party. Also standing in the way of annexation and potential statehood was Babcock himself, whose reputation as a shady character was already becoming entrenched. Congress assumed that if Babcock were in the mix, something had to be amiss. Rumors began to circulate that while Babcock was negotiating on behalf of the United States, he was also negotiating on behalf of Babcock. It hardly needs to be stated that speculators interested in Dominican did not have the well-being of the former slaves in mind. Babcock's ties to these speculators led to suspicions that an unstated clause in the treaties awarded some of the island's more attractive areas for development to Babcock himself. So persuasive were these rumors that Congress launched an investigation into the secretary's affairs.

As would be the pattern in Babcock's life, he maintained just enough plausible deniability to avoid conviction. But if a sense of indignation should arise over this injustice, it is mitigated by the fact that Grant's personal secretary seldom seemed to profit from his get-rich schemes, which more often than not blew up in his face.

But at last, it seemed, the authorities had Babcock dead to rights in yet another Grant administration scandal that became known as the Whiskey Ring in which a broad network of scofflaws conspired to swindle the government out of millions of dollars in liquor taxes. The Whiskey Ring is regarded as the most serious of the Grant administration scandals, which is saying something, since his underlings were so naughty that on the Internet today it is actually possible to find sets of Grant-scandal flashcards.

The ring was operative through the first half of the 1870s, although this was hardly the first time liquor taxes had been a bone of contention in the United States; as president, George

Washington had led troops against western distillers in the Whiskey Rebellion—among Washington's many skills was compartmentalization, since he himself was owner of the nation's largest producers of hooch. The primary base of operations for the ring was St. Louis, and it ostensibly began as a vehicle for funding Grant's political machine. As usual, this was news to Grant who, quite earnestly it appears, launched an investigation of the ring as soon as he got wind of it, not realizing the trail would lead right to his very doorstep.

The government had tried to crack the ring in the past, without success because the ring always seemed to know ahead of time when an investigation was about to take place. Understanding that there was a snitch high up on the inside, the Treasury Department went to "black ops," creating new codes and sending sensitive dispatches by post instead of wire. To determine whether producers were illegally distilling at night (providing the excess of liquor to be sold untaxed), T-Men were sent to stake out the factories. They were able to affirm nighttime operations before the distillers discovered they were being watched, at which point they sent out a gang of toughs to beat the stuffing out of the informants. But the person who really blew the lid off the ring was an otherwise nondescript business reporter for the *St. Louis Democrat* named Myron Colony, whose face was so familiar in the city commercial scene that distillers, shippers, and tax collectors happily and accurately answered all his questions about production, sales, and tax receipts, not realizing that by doing so they were cooking their own goose.

Unfortunately for Grant, as the tapestry of corruption began to unravel, all threads led to Babcock. The arrests began in May 1875, netting three hundred people in multiple cities across the country. On the first day of the sting, sixteen of the nation's largest distilleries were seized, with many more to follow. Writing in the *North American Review* just six months after the fact, H.V. Boynton said the industry had been caught by complete surprise, all their early-warning systems having failed them: "The whiskey ring of the country recognized the complete overthrow of its fraudulent business. It turned frantically toward the officials it had controlled, and who had shielded and saved it so long, only to find them helpless. It appealed to the politicians to whom it had rendered previous service, to find that scarcely one of them dared even to write or telegraph on the subject."

The connection to the White House went through Grant's army buddy, General John McDonald, the Treasury Department's supervisor of internal revenue for the St. Louis area. McDonald confessed, pointing the finger at Babcock, whom he had kept well compensated to assure that the administration would look the other way. This was a terrible offense to Babcock's honor of course, and he immediately demanded a trial before a military court (where, not coincidentally, he still had a number of close buddies) to clear his good name. But the civilian courts beat him to it, and in December he was indicted to stand trial in St. Louis. Grant was despondent at the news, but he swallowed hard and called for justice to fall where it may—until Babcock got ahold of him, and convinced the president that Treasury Secretary Benjamin H. Bristow was leading a fraudulent investigation to embarrass Grant and secure the Republican nomination for himself. Offered these alternative facts, Grant brightened and chose to invest in them with gusto. He fired the government's special prosecutor John Henderson and brazenly declared that he would take the train to St. Louis and testify to his secretary's innocence in person. This clearly horrified his cabinet members, who, if they couldn't shake Grant's confidence in Babcock, were at least able to steer him away from the public spectacle that testifying in person would have created. There was already enough excitement to go around without that.

The newspapers could barely contain their glee. The nation's scoundrel laureate might have artfully dodged any number of other prosecutions, but this time they had him dead to rights. The *New York Herald* called it a "terrible indictment," and "Babcock's bête noire." National excitement over the trial was at a fever pitch—a spectacle on the order of a nineteenth-century O.J. As the date approached, each train from Washington that chugged into St. Louis was surrounded by throngs of people hoping it might be the one delivering Babcock to meet his fate. So too was the outrage palpable over the firing of Henderson, of which there would be echoes a century later with Richard Nixon's Saturday Night Massacre dismissal of Watergate special prosecutor Archibald Cox. The new prosecutor, meanwhile, tried to assure everyone of his independence by boldly declaring that he would "convict Babcock before any jury of Missourians or I'll quit the state."

Poor Babcock by this time was sorely lacking in the friends department. The government was out to get him, the public despised him, and even his partners in crime had abandoned him like rats, hoping that by implicating Babcock they could save themselves. The *Herald* wrote that "the strangest feature in the case is that is the whiskey 'ring' are quite overjoyed at

Babcock's indictment. All spirit of mutual help has vanished. The ring is in a state of complete disintegration, 'each for himself and the devil for them all,' as the old proverb says."

In fact, it seemed there was only one person associated with the sordid affair who remained loyal. Happily for Babcock, this was the man whom many Americans still remembered as the general who won the Civil War. Grant gave a deposition in defense of his friend, but even so it might have been dawning on him that his trust had been misplaced. Those close to the president noted that the man famous for never forgetting any detail of many of his many military campaigns was suddenly possessed of gaps in his memory that you could wheel a cannon through. He certainly had to have read of the evidence against his chief of staff, including a fistful of telegrams in which Babcock had apparently communicated with members of the ring, telling them to lay low or advising that the coast was clear. However, Grant repeatedly said under oath he couldn't recall critical conversations, or if he could that he hadn't grasped the significance.

It was not Grant's finest performance, but in the end it was enough. As the *New Orleans Bulletin* noted, the case was no longer about Babcock, it was about Grant. The jury of Missouri citizens, which prosecutors had been so confident of, acquitted Babcock in late February. Outside the courthouse, Babcock spoke happily for half an hour on his own personal virtues and related topics. His friends, who had been so silent before, now burst forth with their congratulations and affirmations that they never once doubted his innocence. Babcock was thoughtful enough to make the stack of telegrams available to the press, which duly printed them.

Even the papers were forced to change their tune a bit now that Babcock, in the eyes of the law at least, was innocent. Still, there were caveats. The *New York Tribune* "Congratulates the country on the acquittal. Every patriotic American would have been mortified to have the President's private secretary convicted of such a charge. Thank heaven the taint of the Whiskey Ring does not go as far as the White House. The trial was severe, fair and satisfactory, but some things were not fully explained." Even the jury seemed to agree. As one juror put it, "I wouldn't say that General Babcock isn't guilty, but we did what we thought was right. There wasn't testimony enough not to leave a doubt. We didn't let our mortal convictions, as you call 'em, have anything to do with it."

Although few bought into Babcock's innocence, the whole embarrassing affair would at least put Babcock in his place—wouldn't it? The *New York World* agreed that Babcock "was like the turkey to whom the hunter remarked after shooting off his leg—he has got away, but he will roost low hereafter."

But laying low was not a Babcock strength. Grant had placed Babcock in charge of public buildings in Washington and tried to reinstate him as his chief of staff, until public outrage at yet another scandal made it clear that this would be a bad idea. And if Grant had figured that a world of builders and developers replete with big contracts and big expenditures would be a safe environment in which Babcock could keep his nose clean, he was sorely disappointed. It was like putting a drunk behind the counter of a liquor store. Just two months after his court victory in St. Louis, the enterprising engineer was once again under indictment.

While the myriad scandals in the Grant administration had their charms, for pure artistry nothing came close to what became known as the Safe-Burglary Conspiracy, which was like all the indiscretions during the breadth of the Nixon administration rolled into one. It was a scandal within a scandal, that even the newspapers had trouble summing up neatly. The *National Republican* described it as "a long, long tale unfolding." The *New York Times* called it "a long and dreary farce." The *Times* awarded it elevated status in a crowded field, saying that "the conspiracy—for such it undoubtedly was—must be considered one of the most ingenious, intricate, and wicked of any which have been brought to light during this era of investigations."

The initial scandal had nothing to do with safes or burglaries, but centered on a Washington public works program that had admittedly modernized the city, but left it hopelessly in debt, either due to overbuilding, graft or, more likely, a healthy combination of the two. At the center of this investigation was the handsome, progressive governor of the District of Columbia, "Boss" Alexander Shepherd.

Shepherd was ahead of his time on issues of civil rights and women's suffrage, and he also had a penchant for, so to speak, capital improvements. The Civil War soldiers who had vacated the city in 1865 had left it a mess—or at least more of a mess. Shanties, muddy streets, and open sewers had people talking seriously of moving the capital to St. Louis, which would have left Washington to die on the vine.

Thanks to Shepherd, that didn't happen. In seemingly no time he had paved 157 miles of roads and sidewalks, and built 123 miles of sewers, 39 miles of gas mains, and 30 miles of water lines. But to make all this progress took a heavy hand. At one point, he became determined to demolish the wretched but popular Northern Liberties Market where many farmers sold their goods and many residents bought their food.

Protests against its destruction fell on deaf ears, and one night, seemingly out of nowhere, a demolition crew appeared with wrecking bars and picks. Shepherd's opponents sought a court injunction, only to learn that the city's lone judge had been taken by one of the Boss's friends that night for a long, relaxing carriage ride in the country. The building came down, with haste being more important than safety. Two people died: a butcher who was too slow to vacate the premises, and a boy who had arrived with his pet terrier to chase some of the thousands of newly homeless rats.

Ultimately though, Shepherd's ideas were bigger than the city's budget, even with exponentially higher taxes. The original building program was budgeted at $6.25 million, but citizens—including some who had been forced to sell property to pay the taxes they owed—suspected it had greatly exceeded even the admitted cost overruns. They petitioned Congress for an audit. A thorough accounting discovered the city to be $13 million in the red, and Congress declared bankruptcy on the city's behalf. Further, some of the construction had been haphazardly performed, and improvements tended to gravitate to areas of the city where Shepherd's friends owned property. Congress abolished Shepherd's position and decided that the city was too be ruled a three-member commission instead of a governor. Remarkably, President Grant nominated Shepherd to one of the three commissioner chairs, an audacious, or at least tone-deaf move that the Senate rejected the same day. All told, it was little wonder the Grant-Shepherd faction felt they would be well served by deflecting attention from matters at hand.

In April 1874, as the House was in the midst of its investigation, the safe of a district attorney assigned to the case was dynamited and some valuable documents, presumably evidence, was removed. Prior to the break-in, however, Richard Harrington, one of Shepherd's attorneys, received (or said he did) a mysterious note warning that the crime was about to be committed. Being the fine, upstanding citizen that he was, Harrington decided to act on the tip, and he, along with the Chief of Police and members of the Secret Service, staked out the DA's office. And what do you know, two burglars did indeed show up, just as Harrington's anonymous snitch had predicted.

The police followed one of the criminals to the house of Columbus Alexander, a prominent Washington citizen who had played a key role in pressing the corruption case against the city government. As the crook was ringing the doorbell, the police pounced. After a rather theatric show of resistance, the fellow gave up and "confessed" that he had blown the safe while in the employ of Mr. Alexander, and that he was making an appearance at the house to collect his pay.

As attempts to frame an enemy go, it was a poor effort. Or, as the *New York Times* said, "the story bore on the face of it many marks of improbability." Alexander's reputation was beyond reproach, and, once examined, the papers taken from the safe appeared to have little relevance to anything associated with the case.

When it became apparent that no one was going to buy the tale, all hands began pointing at each other, and eventually

Harrington and Secret Service Director Hiram Whitley were indicted. But so confused was the testimony—"there was a great deal of hard swearing in the course of the trials, and it was clear that perjury had been committed by some of the witnesses," the *Times* wrote—that convictions were out of the question, and the indictments were quashed.

The trials had taken eight months and resulted in a whole lot of nothing. Everyone seemed willing to forget the whole thing, except for Mr. Alexander, who was still quite piqued at the ham-handed attempt to smear his good name.

Curiously, one of the safe robbers, George Miles, was worried about his good name as well. It wasn't that he minded so much being accused of criminal activity, but so comedic was the Safe-Burglary fiasco, that apparently the criminal underworld was treating him as something of a buffoon, and Miles was tired of it. Even a crook has his reputation to look out for, and if he doesn't do it, who will? Miles, while in a Vermont jail on an unrelated charge, wrote to Congress and complained that he had "borne the stigma of that notorious Washington safe burglary already too long."

To clear his name, Miles said he was working at the behest of Whitley, and that the whole shebang was the brainchild of Harrington and President Grant's most trusted, if that's the word, assistant Orville Babcock.

For Babcock, certainly it was a new low—not because anyone felt him incapable of vice, but because the Gold Ring and Whiskey Ring, to cite two examples out of many, contained respectable amounts of cunning. The *Times* deemed the Safe-Burglary affair as too stupid for even a cheap detective novel: "If some such story as this here outlined were right out in a drama, it would be considered wildly improbable. Such a mass of perjury, chicanery and general wickedness is rarely put together in any of the modern romances of crime."

All of Washington seemed to be of one mind: Babcock may have skated in the past, but this time he had been caught dead to rights. The question became, what did Babcock know and when did he know it? Leaned upon, Whitley also pointed the finger at Babcock.

Whitley, like Gilbert and Sullivan's model of a modern major gentleman, had started his career as a grocer and a failed Pike's Peak prospector who, through no great talent on his part, found himself appointed to become the chief of the United States Secret Service. Whitley was a Confederate sympathizer until it proved convenient not to be, and he had successfully ducked military service by captaining a Red River steamship. When the Confederates commandeered his boat for the purposes of sinking it as a barrier to Union advancement, Whitley accurately read this scheme as a sign that the North might be getting the upper hand, so he stole a rowboat and threw his lot in with the Yankees at New Orleans.

The provost marshal there employed Whitley as a detective, and the former grocer was appointed by Grant to head the Secret Service in 1869. In this position, and with no particular moral compass to trouble him, Babcock found Whitley useful in a variety of odd-jobs, some of which sound remarkably familiar to modern political ears. The *Times* reported that "Babcock informed Whitley that the New York papers were using his name unjustly in connection with District matters generally, and he wanted Whitley to get a man to circulate among the correspondents and ascertain who was responsible."

Although he was cleared, sort of, in the recent Whiskey Ring scandal, everyone felt that this time there was no way the slippery Babcock could escape any more scandals, particularly since Grant by this time surely had gotten wise to the ways of his wily friend.

On April 10, 1876, just a week before Babcock would be indicted yet again, the Chicago Tribune wrote hopefully that "there is good authority for the statement that the president has discovered that he has been deceived by Babcock and others in very many things during the course of his administration, and that he will soon take occasion in some decisive way to convince the public of this fact."

Grant at this time was still popular, but it was clear his administration was dragging him down, in the eyes of the public. No one trusted Babcock or the nascent Secret Service—today's "so-called judges" might take heart that the papers in the 1860s were referring to the "so-called Secret Service." And while Alexander Shepherd might not have been the most honest guy around, he was given something of a pass because, at least in the eyes of citizens and the press, no one could argue he didn't have Washington's best interests at heart.

Although in the Whiskey Ring episode, Babcock had benefitted from friends in high places, friends in low places would win him his freedom in the Safe-Burglary case. The jury chose to believe Babcock over the rogues' gallery of accomplices whom his defense attorneys, with reason, said were not to be trusted as they one by one implicated Babcock in order to save their own hides. Beyond that, many felt the jury had been tampered with. Whatever the case, Babcock was able to clear his last legal hurdle with scarcely a scratch. The

Memphis Daily Appeal threw up its hands as it wrote, "Once again Babcock has escaped. Boss Shepherd and his administration were more than a match for justice. They took advantage of the blindfolded jade, and weighted the scales as they listed."

Babcock continued on in government jobs through the years, finally being named Inspector of Lighthouses by President Rutherford B. Hayes. He continued in this capacity until 1884 when, working on the Mosquito Inlet Lighthouse off the coast of Florida, he fell overboard during a storm and drowned. He was forty-eight. After years of corruption, it was honest work that finally killed him.

CHAPTER 8

The First Woman in Congress

On a frigid January day in 1968, five thousand women dressed in black shivered in the snow on the foot of Capitol Hill. Their ranks, according to the *New York Times*, included "gray-haired grandmothers, chic suburban house-wives, miniskirted teenagers—they had come by plane, by train, by bus to petition Congress on opening day to withdraw all American troops from Vietnam."

The concourse at Union Station was packed with women, fourteen-hundred of whom had been enticed by a special $7.50 round trip train ticket from New York City. Some came from the big cities of Philadelphia, Boston, and Cleveland. Others were from small towns in Appalachia. They came from both coasts and from the heartland, and they carried banners advertising the states where they were from, to the point, the *Times* noted, that the passenger station resembled a political convention. In the march were Mrs. Dagmar Wilson of Washington, founder of Women Strike for Peace; at her side was Coretta Scott King, just ten weeks away from becoming a widow.

But there was no doubt who was leading this female tour de force. That honor went to eighty-seven-year-old Jeannette Rankin, who more than a half century prior had become the first woman elected to Congress, an event that was all the more remarkable because her election predated the Nineteenth Amendment that gave women nationally the right to vote.

The women with their banners and petitions were intent on taking their grievances directly to Congress, but there was a problem. In 1882, Congress had grown sick and tired of the great unwashed trampling its grounds, advancing agendas, hawking patent medicine, and making a general nuisance of itself. So it passed The Act to Regulate the Use of the Capitol Grounds, which limited foot traffic to designated walkways and prohibited, among other things, "any harangue or oration," and made it a crime to "parade, stand, or move in processions or assemblages, or display any flag, banner, or device designed or adapted to bring into public notice any party, organization, or movement."

The law was old, but it had a number of notches in its pistol, having stymied Coxey's Army of unemployed citizens in 1894, and more than a century later thwarted, temporarily at least, kids who wanted to sled on Capitol Hill after a snowstorm.

As police closed ranks on Jeanette Rankin and her followers she made it clear she would not suffer the same fate as Jacob Coxey. "There is no reason why old ladies shouldn't be allowed to go into the Capitol," she pronounced. As folk artist

Judy Collins sang "This Land is Your Land," Rankin and a small delegation of her followers were allowed inside the congressional halls to personally deliver their petition to House Speaker John McCormack and Senate Majority Leader Mike Mansfield. By all accounts, Rankin was treated with dignity and respect, which hadn't always been the case.

Jeannette Rankin was born in the Montana territory in 1880, the daughter of a school teacher and a rancher who, out of nowhere created quite the political family—her brother would go on to be a powerful player in the Republican Party, and eventually would sit on the Montana Supreme Court. On the ranch, Rankin's chore list included the standard domestic fare, but also demanded that she be a mechanic, farmer, and carpenter. At that point, it began to dawn on her that she was doing the work of men and taking on the responsibilities of men, in a world where women were forced to accept second-rate privileges and were not even allowed to vote. Still, she earned a college degree and began a career in social work that naturally gravitated toward women's and children's issues. But that would change.

In 1887, the US Senate had taken up the issue of women's suffrage. Henry Blair, a senator from New Hampshire, argued passionately for the cause. He advanced the idea that while men might be physically superior, women had the mental edge: "If, then, there be a distinction between the souls of human beings resulting from sex, I claim that, by the report of the minority and the universal testimony of all men, woman is better fitted for the exercise of the suffrage than man."

Curiously, this "women are smarter" argument failed to persuade a chamber full of old male coots, and the resolution failed by a vote of 34–16. This rejection at the national level sent suffragists to the states, where they worked for incremental change. Here they met with success, particularly in the West, where women such as Rankin were more accustomed to working alongside of men, and the population in general was younger and perhaps more adventurous. In 1869, Wyoming became the first state (loosely defined, Wyoming still being a territory at the time) to give women the vote. A number of interesting stories/explanations for the vote have filtered down through the years, but the best by far is the account of Edward M. Lee, a Civil War veteran from Connecticut who was appointed secretary of Wyoming Territory by President Grant in 1869, and swore that the whole affair began as one big fat gag. He later wrote, "Once, during the session, amid the greatest hilarity, and after the presentation of various funny amendments and in the full expectation of a gubernatorial veto, an act was passed Enfranchising the Women of Wyoming. The bill, however, was approved, became a law, and the youngest territory placed in the van of progress. How strange that a movement destined to purify the muddy pool of politics should have originated in a joke."

Another account holds that the vote was a calculated move to attract women to the territory, which could then apply for statehood once certain population thresholds were met. A perhaps more plausible explanation is that the Republicans voted for it in hopes of embarrassing the Democrats, while the Democrats voted for it in hopes of embarrassing the Republicans. In the end, no one was willing to be the bad guy, and the measure sailed through even though it was not exactly at the top of anyone's agenda. When the dust had settled, women had the vote for the first time in America, and befuddled Wyoming politicians were left to accept telegrams of congratulations from the likes of Susan B. Anthony and leaders around the world from Britain to Prussia.

Utah, Colorado, and Idaho followed suit. Rankin by this time was living in Seattle, attending the University of Washington and working as a "baby placer" finding homes for orphaned children. She was also working as a lobbyist for the National American Women Suffrage Association in 1910, when Washington State came aboard. It was in this campaign that Rankin discovered she had a gift for public speaking and organization that few other women of her era could match. A year later, Rankin became the first woman to speak before the Montana legislature, asking a sea of men to give women the vote, which, three years later, they did.

By this time, war clouds were forming over Europe, and if there were an issue Rankin cared about as deeply as suffrage, it was pacifism. In fact, she would have had difficulty separating the two. It was callous male leadership that drew nations into war to begin with. But this wasn't anything Rankin could influence outside of Congress—this was a mission that called for an inside job. Although her candidacy for representative from the state of Montana seemed to take America by surprise, she had become a figure on the national scene by the mid-teens, having successfully led state suffrage campaigns and lobbied extensively in Congress on behalf of women and children. Her reputation was such that she commanded a standing ovation when she appeared to speak at assembly halls across the country. The skills she had learned working to give women the vote would play well in a race for public office.

Rankin threw her hat into the ring for a Montana congressional seat in 1916, with an agenda of peace, suffrage, family issues, and prohibition. The way she saw it, farm animals were getting better representation in Congress than were women and children. She noted that "Several years ago, during one session of Congress, $300,000 was appropriated for the study of fodder for hogs, and at the same session only $30,000 was appropriated for the study of the needs of the nation's children. If the hogs of the nation are ten times more important to men than the children of the nation, it is high time women should make their influence felt in Congress."

From day one it was clear that the male establishment had no clue how to deal with a female candidate, so for the most part they just didn't. Newspapermen who were handed her campaign materials looked at it as if they had just been handed a baby squid. "Women couldn't even vote in most states, so journalists must have thought it ludicrous for a woman to seek election to Congress," wrote Maria Braden in her book *Women Politicians and the Media*. "Even the *New York Times* thought it such a dim possibility that editors returned Rankin's biographical material before the election."

To some degree, it's possible that this negative reaction worked to Rankin's advantage. Had her candidacy been taken more seriously, more interests might have worked against her. She ran as a Republican because she came from a family of Republicans, but her political philosophy was far from conservative orthodoxy. The politically powerful mine owners suspected, and not without cause, that Rankin sympathized with labor, and she hardly spoke for the GOP establishment in regard to her pacifism and advocacy for children's and women's issues. Not that it mattered, since she would never be elected.

But Rankin's snub at the hands of the business and the press did something else: It forced her and her supporters to get the message out themselves instead of through traditional channels. And, after all the suffrage campaigns, she knew how to organize and how to win. "She is a red-hot campaigner," wrote the *Evening Star*. "One of her stunts was to make speeches in the dance halls of the mining towns and then dance on the dancing floors with the miners for partners." Back and forth across the state she and a small army of women supporters trudged. They knocked on doors, mailed postcards, and took advantage of a budding technology, namely a carbon granule transmitter coupled with an electromagnetic receiver that would come to be called the telephone. On Election Day, this grassroots campaign paid off, and newspapers had to tear up the type on their front pages telling the story of a Rankin defeat. "Don't you feel elated over what you have accomplished?" Rankin asked her supporters. "This was not my campaign. The splendid vote I received and the hearty reception which I have been given throughout the state during the campaign are simply demonstrations of the determination of Montana women to have a woman represent them in Congress."

Rankin's election shook the nation and led to one of the great love-hate relationships of her time. "After the election results were in, there was a dramatic shift in the way newspapers dealt with Rankin," Braden wrote. "The press couldn't get enough of her. Reporters and photographers camped out at her house in Missoula. Advertisers wanted endorsements for their products: An auto business offered her a free car and a toothpaste firm offered her $5,000 for a photo of her teeth." About the only person not caught up in the gaiety was Jeannette's brother Wellington, who was taking a brutal ribbing from his mates because he too had run for Congress a few years prior—and lost.

Suddenly, everyone wanted to know who this history-making woman was. The epithet "fake news" wouldn't be coined for another century, but stories began to pop up about Rankin that had very little basis in reality. The peaceful, diminutive brunette was transmogrified into a rootin' tootin' tall, leggy redhead from the Wild West, coming to the nation's capital with six-shooters ablazing.

After the press went through its Annie Oakley phase, it set out to paint a portrait of her as a harmless, nonthreatening woman who understood her place. Yes, she might have gotten out of her lane by running for Congress, but she could, when no one was looking, sew her own hats and she could dance like a lady and "has won genuine fame among her friends with the wonderful lemon meringue pie she makes when she hasn't enough other things to keep her busy."

She was lauded for being an "expert bread maker" who "makes her own clothes" and "loves little children" and "fox-trotted into the hearts of the male voters of Montana." While the papers tended to treat suffragists with suspicion, they gave Rankin a pass because she was "a dainty bit of femininity" who did not have the butch appearance of other troublemakers. The *Watkins Syndicate* wrote, "She is none of your old-school 'women's rights' agitators of the comic cartoons of a generation ago, with hair whacked tight in a French pea behind the ears." So she had that going for her.

But newspapermen who fixated on her appearance were missing a far bigger picture. Rankin had been broadly educated at a number of top universities, and might have been considered one of the nation's leading scholars on families and family economics. Prior to her election, she had taken a three-month trip to New Zealand to study progressive reforms and see how they worked. Rankin was about as prepared for the national stage as a person could be, even as the press continued to focus on her dancing abilities.

Rankin and her intellect had their defenders. Some predicted that male lawmakers would ignore her acumen at their peril. A Montana professor predicted, "They will find in their midst not that impulsive, irrational, sentimental, capriciously thinking and obstinately feeling being which many imagine women to be, but a strong and well-balanced personality, scientifically trained, accustomed to strict reasoning, well versed in the art of politics, inspired by high social ideals, tempered by wide experience."

And Braden noted that the Louisville *Courier-Journal* applauded her courage, asking how a man might feel if he were alone in a room with 434 women. But mostly Rankin was viewed as a novelty, and the launching pad for early twentieth-century comedy acts. Many found Christopher Morley's ditty in the *New York Times Magazine* uproariously funny:

We'll hear no more of shabbiness,
Among our legislators.
She'll make them formal in their dress;
They'll wear boiled shirts and gaiters.

But Rankin and her female supporters knew that her term in office would be no laughing matter, and that she would be intensely watched, not just by women in her home state, but by women across the country. Showing more perception than most, a correspondent to the *Sunday Star* reported that women "know that the wrong woman if selected as America's first congresswoman would do irreparable harm to the suffrage cause. Miss Rankin appreciates that her every movement in the House of Representatives will be watched, and that a thousand tongues will be ready to criticize her every act to disparage the house of woman suffrage."

Truth be told, no one knew quite what to expect at the imminent infiltration of the ultimate Boys Club, but all of Washington was abuzz and no one wanted to miss the show. The *Evening Star* wrote in November 1916, "There isn't anything in connection with the organization of the House that is going to attract as much attention as the maiden speech of the first woman member of the national legislature." The House floor had seen its share of outcasts and misfits, from ranting socialists to nagging prohibitionists, but when Rankin spoke, the *Star* predicted "the doorkeeper will have to issue tickets." One writer said it would "be the most interesting moment around the Capitol since Ben Johnson plugged John Shields in the jaw, or since 'Buck' Kilgour of Texas kicked the door in."

There seemed to be as much speculation about how the "Maid of Missoula" would drain the swamp and turn Washington on its ear as there was prior to the inauguration of Donald Trump. Finally, the papers said, the Speaker would have an ally in his losing battle to keep members from putting their feet on their desks. "There is plenty of reason to believe," wrote the *Star*, "that the manners of the cloakroom loungers will have to be improved or Representative Jeannette Rankin will arise to a point of personal privilege and bawl out some perfectly inoffensive member for failing to hit the cuspidor in the regular afternoon target match between old friends."

In (very slight) defense of male reporters trying to wrap their brains around a female member of Congress; by writing of Rankin's clothing and appearance they were only trying to give female readers what they assumed they wanted. One reporter for the *Evening Star* even apologized in advance for not being up to the job when covering Rankin's first day in office: "Far be it from an ordinary, hard-working reporter of the masculine persuasion to put into this story the feminine touches for which women readers, yea, even the militant suffragists will search." The writer probably should have followed his initial instinct, but in the end he couldn't help himself by noting, "The first congresslady of the United States was arrayed in what seemed to be one of those gauzy things, blue and black, with some more gauzy stuff pinch hitting in place of real material in the bosom of the gown. She carried a big bunch of some kind of flowers—it wasn't possible to see just what they were—and she looked like just what she was, a real woman in the midst of a lot of men, the first woman ever to occupy a seat there by virtue of the suffrage of her fellow citizens, and perhaps a little nervous about it all."

To their credit, House members gave Rankin a warm welcome. A breakfast was held in her honor, and supporters and opponents of the suffrage movement alike want out of their way to greet her. Rankin had to do so much polite smiling and bowing, that reporters feared her facial muscles might seize, and when her name was called by the clerk at roll call, she was given an ovation that lasted several minutes.

And there she might have left it, and she might have remained a freak-show heroine and a star in the mold of a female figurehead—sewing, dancing, and baking lemon pies—had she not had the audacity to have her own views, and the conviction to stick to them. It was in this respect that the male establishment appeared to get truly agitated. Rankin was effectively given no time to gently assimilate herself into the congressional way of life before the most consequential issue of the new century came to a vote—entry into World War I. All pretenses of lightheartedness and mirth disappeared when Rankin voted no.

Braden called it a "cruel irony" that this was the first vote Rankin was called on to make, accentuated because it was cast during a special session of Congress. No fool, the nation's first congresswoman understood the situation. She would be scrutinized as no other member would be, and she knew her convictions would prevent her from being on the right side of both history and popular opinion. "I want to stand by my country, but I cannot vote for war," she said, fighting back tears. The clerk asked her to be clear; was she voting against the resolution? Faintly, Rankin acknowledged this to be the case, before sinking back into her seat. She was not alone; forty-nine other representatives joined her, and many of them were blinking back tears as well. History did not record, or at least make a big deal of, any men who were emotionally moved by the magnitude of the moment.

But the first woman to sit in Congress got no such pass. She was "weeping," or "sobbing," or even "fainting." The papers didn't focus on her principles; they focused on, and greatly accentuated, her demeanor. It took an incredible amount of strength to vote the way she did, yet the papers went out of their way to make her look weak. And it was a hint of how she would be treated in the future.

But for the time being, her novelty still made for good press, so she was not about to be run out of town. Specifically, her fans and critics alike were holding out for the summer of 1917 when she would make her first scheduled speech on the floor of the House. By this time, Rankin had some time under her belt as a representative, and there would be no repeat of her shaky performance the previous year. It was a good thing, since her speech was scrutinized like no other at the time.

One and all expected the congresswoman to speak on her pet topic, awarding women the vote. But once again, she was about to surprise her observers.

Through the early part of the twentieth century, labor issues had been on a low boil, waiting to explode. In Rankin's neck of the woods, this pertained to the copper mines that produced metals that had become all the more important as the nation had joined the fight in Europe. The unions were fighting the mine owners, but they were also fighting each other. Former Idaho Governor Frank Steunenberg had been assassinated in 1905 by Harry Orchard, a union member who was also a paid informant of the Cripple Creek Mine Owners Association. Orchard confessed, but said that three members of the radical Western Federation of Miners had put him up to it. The WFM leadership was arrested and put on trial in what would become one of the more celebrated cases of the era. Orchard would spend the rest of his life in jail, but the three WFM leaders were acquitted after their attorney, the transcendent Clarence Darrow, called more than a hundred witnesses and gave a closing argument that lasted the better part of two weeks.

But the case accentuated a festering division between the WFM and the Industrial Workers of the World, with growing unease on the part of miners that their leadership was too prone to violence. The stalemate between the two unions played into the hands of the mine owners, as more western mines operated as open shops. Not surprisingly, mine owners were more than happy to take advantage of the situation, blackballing men who had union proclivities on one side or the other. Two months after Congress had voted to go to war, miners were lowering a twelve-hundred-foot electric cable into the deep Speculator copper mine outside Butte, Montana. The cable slipped and became entangled in the middle of the shaft, and when a foreman went to inspect, his carbide lamp set the cable's insulation on fire, and—lacking any semblance of safety precautions—at least 163 men died of asphyxiation.

The miners struck for better conditions, and when the mining companies refused to negotiate, the men discovered that in Jeannette Rankin they had a champion. So the first speech from a female representative in the history of the United States did not deal with the disenfranchisement of women, it dealt with the plight of male miners. "Contrary to expectations," wrote the *Washington Times*, "and to the amazement of the women who had turned out to hear the lady from Montana [her speech] was a plea for the battling miners of the West and not an argument for women suffrage."

Pretty much everyone in attendance was caught off guard. She had entered the chamber "with every congressman gallantly on his feet and thunderous applause swelling up from the floor to the galleries, which were packed as never before with more than 600 women," the *Times* reported. Many of the men who had been applauding Rankin pretty quickly thought better of it. The paper noted that "it was obvious from the moment Miss Rankin began to speak that her resolution would arouse tremendous antagonism." Rankin noted that the mines were running roughshod over the men, driving out union men and even lynching dissenters.

This was too much for one western lawmaker who jumped to his feet and asked whether Rankin knew the track record of the man who was dispatched. "To me it is a question of lawlessness and not a question of who was hanged," Rankin snapped, to the applause of the people in the galleries.

The lawmaker leaped back to his feet to make the point that the dead man was a member of the unions implicated in the assassination of Governor Steunenberg. "Do you think these men who boast that they know no allegiance to the United States or any other country have any right to squeal when one of their number gets hanged?" The audience roared with laughter, but Rankin, the papers noted, "having said her say and evidently realizing the futility of a verbal battle, remained seated in dignified and somewhat contemptuous silence."

In a year, Rankin had come a long way. Gone was the deferring, uncertain woman who had been so unsure of her own vote a year ago. She had come to the chamber late, as all the men did, and held jocular court with a number of her colleagues before rising to speak. Her high voice carried well in the chamber and, said the *Times*, "Contrary to the usual custom during set speeches, practically every member remained to listen to what Miss Rankin had to say."

The nation would continue to hang on Rankin's every word, in good ways and bad. She was frequently in the papers, and often made the front page. If she championed an issue it was bound to get the attention of the press in ways that the common male congressman could only dream of. Unfortunately for Rankin, it seemed that once the shiny newness wore off of her position, the press went out of its way to take potshots. In the tradition of American celebrity, it seemed that Rankin was elevated to great heights only to be yanked back to earth. In the summer of 1917, the *Washington Times* ran a snarky front-page story gleefully headlined "Montana Women Bitterly Attack Jeannette Rankin." To the press, the ultimate indictment of a woman was for her to be criticized by members of her own pack, giving her a "figurative hair-pulling": "Armed with sharp tongues, many of the fair ones who supported Miss Jeannette Rankin, now Congresswoman, were outspoken today in declarations that her nation in coming [to Montana] to investigate labor conditions is merely a sensational move to annex labor votes in her announced race against Senator A. J. Walsh."

Rankin had scarcely been in office a year when Montana split its single congressional district into two, and placed her in the Western part of the state where she understood she would face little chance of reelection. In order to retain her statewide base, she decided to run for the Senate. Her likely opponent, Thomas J. Walsh, was a follower of President Woodrow Wilson, which in Rankin's eyes made him a sell-out to the war effort. Walsh, a Democrat who would die in office, was a progressive politician who had already staked out a lot of the ground Rankin hoped to claim. In the end, she didn't even get the chance to face him directly when she was defeated in a crowded primary.

The first woman member of Congress was popular as long as she was a winner, but when she lost, out came the knives. She "bit off more than she could chew," cackled one reporter. A column on the front page of the *New York Times* was particularly savage. "Hailed as a glory of feminism by the feminists after her election, her political career in the House and in her state is an awful example. . . . Miss Rankin should never have gone into politics. Her judgment is feebly developed in comparison with her sentimentality."

Out of office, Rankin continued to work for peace, consumer affairs, family issues and for a constitutional amendment banning child labor. She never married, nor even seemed to have time for a personal relationship. She spent her days on a small farm in Georgia, where she founded a pacifist organization and spent the next two decades lobbying Congress on matters close to hear heart.

By 1940, she returned to Montana where she again won election to Congress, and again found herself swallowed up by a growing agitation for war. This time, when the Japanese bombed Pearl Harbor, she herself was also on an island. A handful of other representatives had shared her view prior to World War I, but not now. Or even if they did, they were not about to admit to that fact in public. Everyone demanded revenge for what President Franklin Roosevelt famously tagged "an unprovoked and dastardly attack" on the American Navy.

Aware of Rankin's peaceful proclivities, her friends, family, and colleagues rushed to her side in an attempt to save her from herself. Americans were raging, and anyone who stood in the way of their bloodlust would be skinned. So frequent and frantic were these entreaties prior to the vote that she finally got into her car and drove the streets of Washington, working up a good lather in the process. When Rankin's turn to vote on the House floor came, all eyes turned her way. She might have justified her opposition to a foreign war overseas, but surely she could not let a direct attack on one of our own military bases go unchallenged. Yet surely she could. The final vote for war was unanimous in the Senate and 388–1 in the House.

At the age of sixty-one, though, there was none of the nervousness or trepidation that had afflicted the young thirty-seven-year-old more than two decades before. As a woman, Rankin calmly explained, she was not allowed to serve in the military, so she could not in good faith vote to send a man to do work in a field that excluded women. It was pacifism seen through the lens of feminism; it was impossible to simultaneously support war and women's rights. It was an interesting intellectual wrinkle, but it didn't save her. The vote, wrote Daniel B. Moskowitz for *World War II Magazine*, "happened just after 1 p.m. on December 8 in the Capitol in Washington, as Irving Swanson, a clerk in the House of Representatives, read members roll call, recording their votes on the fateful resolution declaring war against Japan. 'Yea' after 'yea' came in like an echo as Swanson read the names at a pace of 20 per minute until he got to Rankin, who in a firm voice announced her stance: 'No.' Other House members began hissing."

After the vote, she was mobbed by the press, to the point she had to take refuge in a phone booth—like a "cornered rabbit," the papers stated—until the Capitol police could be summoned to lead her to safety. By some accounts the phone booth was pummeled with tomatoes, although it might be a stretch to think reporters or anyone else were in the habit of carrying tomatoes on their person should someone at any given time be deserving of a good pummeling.

But fruit might have been preferable to the onslaught of fetid words hurled her way. Almost immediately, the telegrams came pouring in. America should open a concentration camp, they said, and Rankin should be Prisoner Number One. Her brother wired that her constituency "is 100 percent against you." Montana Republican National Committeeman Dan Whetstone begged Rankin to "redeem Montana's honor" by changing her vote. "Messages from all parts of Montana indicate disappointment over your attitude in failing to support the war declaration," he told her by telegraph. Even the rival Kiwanis and Rotary clubs of tiny Dillon, Montana, set aside any simmering service club differences to pen a joint letter of rebuke.

Back in her office, Rankin issued a statement that discreetly avoided the feminist angle: "I believed that such a momentous vote—one which would mean peace or war for our country—should be based on more authentic evidence than the radio reports now at hand. Sending our boys to the Orient will not protect this country. . . . Taking our army and navy across thousands of miles of ocean to fight and die cannot come under the heading of protecting our shores."

It was a rather weak and disjointed assessment, not that it mattered. Rankin's move had branded her a traitor, and there was nothing she could do about it. Three days later, when a vote was taken on war with Germany and Italy, the effects of this public browbeating were apparent. She recorded herself as present but not voting, doing so in a voice so faint the clerk asked her to repeat herself.

Rankin had her supporters, but they tended to come in small, marginalized groups on the fringes. On December 12, six people were arrested in Los Angeles after leading a meeting of pacifists in which Rankin was given a standing ovation for her vote in opposition of the war. The leader was Robert K. Noble, a radio personality and leader of a California pension plan known as the Ham and Eggs movement—so called because old people at breakfast would be able to move up from gruel to ham and eggs. Along with honoring Rankin, Noble, told the crowd that the Pearl Harbor attack had been faked, and urged the impeachment of Roosevelt. With friends like this, Rankin scarcely would have needed enemies.

But at root, Rankin did not budge. "You cannot have war and democracy," she said. You cannot have war and liberty. After this political conflagration, however, Rankin lost her zeal for office. Her name stopped showing up on legislation, and by the time her term was up, she seldom even showed up for floor votes. Her view of the world was growing more conspiratorial, and she blamed "British imperialists" and FDR's sanctions against Japan as sinister components of war.

Rankin knew better that to run for reelection in 1942. Too much water was over the dam, and her skills were better suited to an outsider than to a member of the club. Coincidentally, Mike Mansfield, who took her seat, was the future senator who would be so gracious to her in another thirty years as she was presenting her petitions protesting the war in Vietnam.

Rankin lived to be ninety-two, dying in 1973. In a tribute to her life published in a Montana paper, an acquaintance said

Rankin had confided to her once that she was curious how history would see her fifty years hence.

Rankin had never heard of a thing called Wikipedia, but it might have interested her to know that her computer-age biography would prominently include this quote, not from some future historian, but from a contemporary, writing in the *Kansas Emporia Gazette* the day after her career-ending vote:

"Probably a hundred men in Congress would have liked to do what she did. Not one of them had the courage to do it. The *Gazette* entirely disagrees with the wisdom of her position. But Lord, it was a brave thing! And its bravery someway discounted its folly. When, in a hundred years from now, courage, sheer courage based upon moral indignation is celebrated in this country, the name of Jeannette Rankin, who stood firm in folly for her faith, will be written in monumental bronze, not for what she did, but for the way she did it."

CHAPTER 9

The Tree at National Cathedral Has a Thorny Past

Entering the city of Washington from the southwest, the driver is treated to a winding, wooded drive on the lush and blossoming George Washington Parkway in Northern Virginia, one of the few parkways that entirely lives up to its billing. The District's celebrated monuments will in time be visible across the Potomac River, but the first iconic silhouette presenting itself is that of the National Cathedral, a spectacular Gothic structure (because, its founders believed, "no other style of architecture is so distinctly Christian as Gothic") soaring to the heavens. It was built of Indiana limestone on Mount St. Alban, four hundred feet above the Potomac. It was designed to appear at a distance to be on the same plane as the top of the Washington Monument. The heavy, massive towers, reaching 220 feet in height, were patterned after the craggy massifs of the Dolomite Mountains in Northern Italy.

The Episcopal founders of the cathedral acknowledged they, architecturally speaking, were walking something of a fine line. They wanted a church that would knock the socks off anyone who saw it, but at the same time they recoiled from excessive ornamentation that might remind anyone of the papacy in Rome. Towers were justified, or rationalized, over spires because European churches on the same latitude had noticed that the thin spires tended to get lost in the low sun. No one wanted the church to be invisible from the government buildings downtown. The architects also made it clear that their Gothic design echoed earlier representations of that particular genre and not the vulgar excesses in design of the late-Gothic period. The architects further carefully considered where every shaft of sunlight and where every shadow would fall inside the great cathedral, accenting the divine and understating the mortal. The main message was one of strength. In the words of its designers, "Christ is the rock of ages and His church is a rock of refuge."

Construction of the cathedral took eight decades, with the final stone being placed in 1990. And from conception to completion, it could be said that the church was two centuries in the works. Washington's designer Pierre L'Enfant had anticipated the need for a "great church for national purposes" as he laid out the city in 1792. It would be the national gathering place for prayer, thanksgiving, funeral orations and such, and partial to no denomination or sect. But even so, the idea for a national church in a country dedicated to the separation of church and state proved unworkable, and the site went for a more secular purpose: a national patent office. But the idea persevered and a century later Congress granted a charter to the Protestant Episcopal Cathedral Foundation which, assisted by President Teddy Roosevelt, laid the cornerstone in 1907.

When the idea for the church was again floated, one of its founders, the Right Reverend Henry Yates Satterlee acknowledged the original concerns about a national church, but couldn't resist noting that it was the state that was more likely to taint the church than the other way around: "Unlike the medieval cathedrals of Europe, with their deep rooted customs and traditions of a united church and state, Washington Cathedral will stand on the firm foundation of a free church in a free state—free from any entangling alliance with government . . . free to hold up the gospel standard of Christ himself amid those evils which honeycomb the social and political life of the capital of every modern nation."

The cathedral is celebrated for its architecture, but also for its world-renowned gardens that were carefully sculpted by Frederick Law Olmsted Jr., son of the man who designed New York's Central Park and gave birth to modern landscape architecture. The younger Olmsted—whose given name was Henry and later changed to Frederick by his father, but everyone called him Rick—remains one of the men whose fingerprints are most upon the Washington cityscape, from the National Mall to Rock Creek Park. To the American Academy of Arts and Letters, Olmsted had "the longest continuing influence of any single individual upon the growth of the Federal City."

Olmsted already had to his credit design work on the White City world exposition in Chicago and the Vanderbilt's sprawling Biltmore estate in Ashville, North Carolina, when in 1901 he took a seat on the five-member McMillan Commission.

It was at the end of the nineteenth century when the artistically minded in the nation's capital decided that its current aesthetic, or lack thereof, just wouldn't do. The architecture, with some inspiring exceptions like the Capitol building and the Smithsonian, was not memorable, and the National Mall had been planted in the Victorian style of closed, shrubby spaces that lent no sense of grandeur. A pedestrian rail station took up space on the mall and worst of all, much of the space north of the mall between the Capitol and White House was populated by a reeking, vice-riddled strip of urban filth known as Murder Bay. L'Enfant, everyone agreed, would be ashamed at what had become of his dream.

The McMillan Commission panel was the product of the Senate Parks Commission and its chairman James McMillan, which unveiled its plan in January 1902. The woods and shrubs of the mall would be replaced with a narrower, but open, grassy expanse flanked by trees, much in the style of Versailles. It would become the heart, or "monumental core" of the city, including tributes to America's heroes, with Murder Bay to be mercifully replaced with handsome government offices, and streets off the mall home to museums, art galleries, and theaters. In addition, a series of parks and gardens were laced throughout the city, connected by parkways on which Washingtonians could reinvigorate themselves with leisurely carriage rides.

Despite political headwinds, the late nineteenth and early twentieth centuries were truly transformative times for the city. The National Zoo, the Lincoln Memorial, and the grand Union Station among many others joined the cathedral in this era. Five years after the McMillan Plan was revealed, Olmsted, at the age of thirty-seven, turned his attention to the Cathedral gardens, a project to which he would devote himself for the next twenty years. It would be among his greatest works.

Olmsted's core belief was that a landscape should work in harmony with its natural setting, and that existing features be worked with to the greatest degree possible. His philosophy was complemented at the cathedral by Florence Bratenahl, wife of the cathedral dean, who was enamored with arches and sculptures and historically significant plantings. In 1916, Mrs. Bratenahl founded the All Hallows Guild, which takes scrupulous care of the cathedral gardens to this day. Together, they crafted and appointed the grounds with judiciously selected plantings, scions of historic shrubbery, sprays of flowers and meticulous stonework to create a sixty-seven-acre cloak of natural beauty that Mrs. Bratenahl said was "a landscape development worthy of Washington Cathedral."

On the seventy-fifth anniversary of the All Hallows Guild, Susan L. Klaus wrote of Olmsted, "He envisioned for this great church a landscape setting of stability, permanence, and dignity. The Cathedral Close is a peaceful oasis in the midst of Washington, a paradise garden that has been nurtured for the past three quarters of a century by those who love it."

No detail was overlooked. Even the density of the leaves of a particular plant, and the amount of sunlight that would filter through to dapple the ground below was considered, along with the shadows that a variety of shrub might cast on an adjoining wall. The effort took time—Olmsted in particular felt a proper landscape could not be rushed, and the initial backbreaking toil of preparing the soil and excavating for future plantings did not always reap immediate aesthetic rewards. From her writings, it appears Mrs. Bratenahl could not always be counted upon to be quite as patient. If a mature tree were available, she was not one to wait on a sapling.

Century-old boxwoods of enormous girth were miraculously dug up and transplanted from a decaying estate seventy-five miles away, as were a half-dozen holly trees up to thirty-five feet high from an abandoned Virginia plantation. Mature holly in particular is notoriously hard to transplant, but the Guild did it, not that this was its most ambitious transplanting project; that honor went to a seventy-five-foot pine that with its root ball weighed in at seventy tons. Workers were somehow able to move this behemoth a fifth of a mile on the cathedral property.

And if specimens came with a story, it was all the better. George Washington—the stone for the gardens was cut from an old Washington quarry—ruminated wistfully on sitting beneath his vine and fig, so it was quite appropriate that a large fig tree was transplanted from Abington, the plantation of Washington's stepson, Jacky Custis. (This is only the second-most-interesting Custis-tree story on record. Custis served under Washington as an emissary to the British, where he befriended a staff member of General William Howe. This officer had on him a cutting from a weeping willow, the first of its kind in England, from the garden of Alexander Pope. The officer planned to plant it on the American lands he was sure the British would capture from the colonists. When it was apparent that wasn't going to work out, he gave the scion to

Custis, and the resulting tree became the parent of every other weeping willow in America.)

For inspiration, the Guild let history be its guide, and not necessarily just recent history, either. One of its greatest coups was the discovery of a plant list from the gardens of Charlemagne, dating back a millennium, which it worked to echo. The gardens contained a box tree transplanted by Thomas Jefferson; a sprig of boxwood from Dolley Madison's inaugural bouquet that was stuck in the ground and took root; yew from old England; roots of ivy that dated to antiquity; and cedars from the Holy Land— all were integrated into the cathedral gardens.

But the gardeners were democratic, and if the best specimen came without pedigree they would not turn it away. Once the perfect magnolia was found improbably growing in the front yard of a shanty near Capitol Hill. The eight-ton, twenty-five-foot tree was loaded onto flatbed to be slowly towed by the biggest truck of its day, escorted by a Ford, a Chevrolet, and a seven-passenger Buick for a phalanx of protection against careless motorists who might for a moment forget themselves at the sight of such an incredible procession.

Mrs. Bratenahl related "the acute difficulties and anxieties of moving so large a tree; especially the unusual operation of literally dropping it over a fifteen-foot wall and sliding it down greased runways to its future home at a forty-five-degree angle. But everything worked out happily and today this beautiful magnolia looks as though it had always been there: utterly peaceful in the midst of continuous turmoil of construction work."

And, of course one man's trash is another man's treasure. A tree on a Maryland farm, a "remarkable box of the dwarf type, though of mammoth size, required a ball of earth eleven and a half feet in diameter for its safe transplanting," Mrs. Bratenahl wrote. The wondrous specimen was thought to date back 250 years and, even more amazingly, have an association with Lord Baltimore. The gardeners who feared the farmer would be reluctant to part with such a prize discovered they needn't have worried when he asked it they could take it within a week, because he wanted to build a new pigsty in its place.

But Mrs. Bratenahl singled out one other amazing tree already on the grounds and flourishing: The Glastonbury thorn tree.

Through the course of human history, few people have been responsible for more good stories than Joseph of Arimathea. Joseph was a wealthy adherent of Jesus, his great uncle it was said, who most famously took possession of Jesus's body after the crucifixion. Joseph had Jesus buried in a tomb he had prepared for himself, but no good deed goes unpunished, and the uncle was accused of grandstanding, and imprisoned by the Jewish elders. His cell was sealed and a guard posted outside, but of course escaping these bonds would be child's play compared to resurrection, and sure enough, the guard and seal were still in place when the authorities discovered Joseph himself was missing. Unlike their ancestors, these elders didn't need a burning bush to determine what was what. They issued an apology and begged him to recount the tale of his escape, which he was more than happy to do. With his base of support broadening, Joseph of Arimathea's career was undeniably fast-tracked. His name is also undeniably musical, and it has stuck through the ages, making him perhaps the only man to have been venerated by the Roman Catholic Church, the

Eastern Orthodox Church, a handful of Protestant churches and Monty Python. Legend holds Joseph as the first keeper of the Holy Grail, and it is through his ties to England and King Arthur that the roots of the Glastonbury thorn tree take hold.

Christ, of course, was issued a crown of thorns by the Romans to cement his humiliation. Joseph of Arimathea happened to cut himself a staff from the same tree that produced the crown as he set about handling his master's funeral arrangements. It took about twelve centuries, but thanks to this one thorn tree everything began to come together for medieval writers looking for ways to explain Christianity's introduction into the British Isles. Glastonbury Abbey, for one, claimed to have been founded by Joseph of Arimethea, which, practically speaking, was a good move, because having been founded by such an important member of Jesus's support staff would add prestige to the church's pedigree, and money to the church's treasury.

The abbey was important and influential in its own right, with significant political and territorial connections, and the story of Joseph only served to stoke the flames. Joseph, legend went, escaped the Holy Land as Christians were increasingly persecuted. He escaped, Holy Grail in tow, with Mary and Martha, their brother Lazarus, and some other disciples who hurriedly boarded a boat with no time to secure such niceties as oars or sails. Thus at the mercy of the wind, they were blown to Marseilles, where Mary, Martha, and Lazarus decided they had enough of the adventure and disembarked. Joseph and a dozen other disciples, however, figured they'd give it one more go and returned to the boat (once again without oars or sails since it worked out well enough the first time) and were blown across channel to England.

The battered party trudged inland until they could go no further—"We are weary all," Joseph reported—and they collapsed in exhaustion atop a knoll that became known as Wearyall Hill. Seeing no place to lean the staff he had cut from the infamous thorn tree, Joseph plunged it into the earth, where it miraculously took root, budded, and bloomed in the dead of winter, the date just happening to be December 25, Christmas Day. The party took this sign to mean that their journey was at an end, and they built a few small huts that become the first Christian mission in the British Isles.

But the journey did not entirely end there, and Glastonbury, centuries later, would come to have ties with the National Cathedral in Washington. The connection was strong enough that at Christmas in 1925, the Very Reverend G. C. F. Bratenahl wrote a spirited defense of the legend of Joseph of Arimathea, which he concluded was just as likely, or more likely, as any other explanation for the spread of Christianity to Britain.

Specifically, he wrote, Joseph was a wealthy trader, who, if pursued, would be familiar with, and likely to follow, standard trade routes, which in that day would have reached Marseilles before angling northwest and across the channel to the tin mines of Britain. It was also recorded that Joseph and his fellow travelers not only were well received upon their arrival in Briton, but they were also given a considerable amount of land for their church (which later and unfortunately burned,), which would indicate that the party already had connections and accounts in the region that would have come from routine trade.

So too did the Holy Grail add credence to the legend, Bratenahl believed. Because while other church relics prolif-erated to the point where "We are told that there are enough bits of the cross to build a ship and enough nails of the cross to fasten it," no other church ever claimed to have a connection with the grail, nor has any other claimed to have been founded by Joseph of Arimathea. Of course, this claim intersects with the legend of King Arthur, said to be buried nearby, and his Knights of the Round Table, who have excited boundless historic and pop culture intrigue.

For the Reverend Bratenahl, there was enough circumstantial evidence to make a good case: "All due allowance is made for the naive and fanciful touches with which a childlike age embroidered its traditions, but the fundamental fact remains that Joseph of Arimathea carried Christianity to Britain in the first century and that the faith which he planted never died."

Not only have the legends not died, they have been expanded upon on American shores, especially at the National Cathedral. Bratenahl noted that the cathedral has three distinct ties to Glastonbury. "There is a Bishop's chair with the following inscription: 'This Glastonbury Cathedra is raised as witness to the continuity of the Anglican Church and presented on Ascension Day, 1901. These stones from the ancient British Abbey of SS. Peter and Paul are given by the churchmen of Glastonbury to the churchmen in America for the Cathedral of SS. Peter and Paul Washington, D.C.'

"The cathedral also has an altar built of stones made from the same ledge of rock as that in which our Saviour's tomb was cut, that is from the historical Joseph of Arimathea's garden." The Reverend couldn't resist noting that should creeping Latinism interfere with church doctrine, "this altar will always . . . remind us that the roots of our Holy Church are in Jerusalem, and that the flower of our faith was transplanted to Britain by one of our Lord's own friends. We look not to the magnificence of Rome for the first fruits of the Anglican faith, but to Glastonbury, where the winter thorn Blossoms at Christmas, mindful of our Lord."

And this was the third connection between Glastonbury and the Washington Cathedral, a graft of the Holy Thorn that was presented to the cathedral at the turn of the twentieth century. In his 1901 book *The Building of a Cathedral*, Henry Yates Satterlee, first Bishop of Washington, wrote that the Glastonbury thorn was "the gift of Mr. Stanley Austin, and an offshoot from the celebrated thorn tree with which so many legends are connected." The Unity Through Diversity project relates that Austin, "son of the then reigning Poet Laureate, owned the Abbey House, with its 'interesting ruins' in the garden. When Stanley heard of the plans to build the National Cathedral in Washington, D.C., he sent a clipping of the Glastonbury Thorn to . . . Satterlee."

Planted at the Cathedral Close outside St. Albans school, the tree flourished, but for sixteen years, it wouldn't bloom. Finally, at Christmas of 1918, the desired blossoms arrived, leading to the conclusion that it had decided to wait out the brutality of the Great War. "Perhaps they had waited for a true Christmas, when the hearts of men should be filled with good will," Bratenahl speculated. The tree lived nearly a century, until according to the All Hallows Guild, it was replaced by scion rooted at the National Arboretum,

The hawthorn tree typically blooms in the spring, but what became known as the Holy Thorn of Glastonbury—an apparent genetic mutation—bloomed twice, once in the spring and once at Christmas. The tree at the Washington Cathedral stayed true to its parent, although many attempts to propagate the tree produced offspring that reverted to the blooming cycle of a standard hawthorn. Not surprising, perhaps, since the hawthorn is a tree of contradictions. The menacing thorns bely what is otherwise an attractive tree, with lush green foliage that is colorful in the fall, cascades of white, pink, or red flowers and small red fruit along the order of crabapple and can be made into jelly. Even in winter, wrote Charles Fenyvesi for the *Washington Post*, "the hawthorn's leafless boughs and twigs outlined against the sky are as articulated as a skeleton, and our eyes are drawn to them as to the rich detail of a Duerer etching that fills every square inch with meaningful motion."

In history, the scent of the flowers has drawn considerable comment. Those who see the glass as half full have associated it with "female fertility," while the half-empty set have used less charitable associations. As such, the Romans associated the blossoms with a ban on sexual intercourse, while to the Turks the hawthorn's branches were an item of erotica. In early Pagan lore, the tree was seen as unlucky—but to cut them down was just begging for a loss of vitality, children, livestock, and property.

Glastonbury itself, oddly enough, has become a pilgrimage not just for Christians, but for pagans, witches, and an eclectic set of individuals attracted by the combination of legend, myth, and history. But not everyone has come in the spirit of love and tolerance that the Holy Thorn has inspired. In 2010, a vandal who was never identified took a chain saw and cut the Holy Thorn down to the trunk.

The Washington Cathedral thorn has an added twist to the legend. Along with blooming every spring and every

Christmas, it was said to bloom, in appreciation of the home-town team, perhaps—every time British royalty visited the city. This built upon a similar legend in Glastonbury proper, when visiting royalty were given petals from the blossoms in a silver box. So too was the Prince of Wales given blossoms in a silver box by Satterlee in 1919, and Princess Elizabeth in 1951. But even before the legend was fueled by the visits of Elizabeth as a princess and again as Queen and by the Queen Mother, not everyone with ties to the cathedral was buying in.

"Of course there is not one chance in a million that St. Joseph of Arimathea planted the historic Glastonbury Tree in England," wrote Anson Phelps Stokes, a resident canon at National Cathedral from 1924 to 1939, and a great philan-thropist but a poor romantic. "Nor is there one chance in a million that there is any connection between the blooming of the tree and the visits of English royalty to Washington." His views were echoed by Dean Francis Sayre, who commented, "I have constantly opposed playing on that old saw ever since I came."

The Glastonbury Thorn might have expected better from men of faith. But from a gardener's perspective, a 2000 All Hallows Guild newsletter, might have put it best when it removed any pressure from the poor tree's thorny shoulders: "The Glastonbury Thorn continues to bloom sometimes at Christmas, sometimes in May or whenever the spirit moves it!"